PRESERVING

FAMILY WEALTH

& Peace of Mind

Estate Planning

Caring for & Communicating to Your Family Through the Legacies You Leave

Loren Dunton and Kim Ciccarelli Banta
The National Center for Financial Education

PROBUS PUBLISHING COMPANY
Chicago, Illinois
Cambridge, England

©1994 NCFE
2200 Sacramento St., Rm 207
San Francisco, CA 94115

This publication is designed to provide accurate and authoritative information in regard to the subject matter covered. It is sold with the understanding that the author and the publisher are not engaged in rendering legal, accounting, or other professional service.

Library of Congress Cataloging in Publication Data Available

ISBN 1-55738-832-6

Printed in the United States of America

BB

1 2 3 4 5 6 7 8 9 0

DEDICATION

This book is dedicated to the memory of Dean,
my friend and beloved husband,
to my family, and to my many clients who
helped provide the research that went
into these chapters.

—KCB

To my wife Marta and all those
in the financial services industry who help
people acquire peace of mind,
the real dividend
from professional financial planning.

—LD

DISCLAIMER

This book is meant as a general reference to guide a person forward in acknowledging responsibility for their legacies and moving ahead with proper estate planning. The information contained herein is deemed reliable based on the sources available at the time of publication. The authors suggest that the reader consult with competent legal, tax, and financial counselors. Individual circumstances may require specific and unique planning solutions. Both spouses should engage in a complete discussion and review, including asset entitlement, family situations, personal preferences, medical circumstances, and estate planning objectives to complete their own definition and method of passing on legacies to their heirs.

Paul Richard, Vice President
National Center for Financial Education

DEFINITIONS

Wealth . . . "resources, assets . . . all property that
has a money or exchange value"

Peace of Mind . . . "freedom from disquieting or
oppressive thoughts and emotions"

Legacy . . . "a gift by will or trust received from an
ancestor or predecessor"

Contents

PART THREE
Observations & Advice from the Professionals

To add interest and value to *Preserving Family Wealth & Peace of Mind: Legacies for You & Your Children,* we invited several financial professionals/associates from across the country, in addition to our own personal network group, to submit observations and information relative to topics this book addresses. Their contributions are as follows:

CONTENTS

CONTENTS

Foreword

The Future Really Starts Now

The United States of America has truly been an upward bull market for its more than 200 years. There certainly have been prominent interruptions based on wars and recessions and even a couple of great depressions, but the overall movement has been upward. We as a nation learned that it is possible to make it without full commitment; there was always a way through; and (recently) many of us learned that it didn't take much to create a living!

That is no longer the case!

This very important book is being written at a crucial moment in which our future is not necessarily guaranteed and many of our traditions and accepted values are at risk.

The average person marrying today for the first time will spend more years caring for parents than raising children, and the average person at the end of his or her life will have had more spouses than children.

This is a dramatic, permanent change in the lifestyles we have grown accustomed to . . . and that our children have witnessed. It is now critically important that each individual create a life-long learning agenda and establish a financial planning program that will make possible not only retirement with dignity, but also passing on important legacies (financial and otherwise) to our children and others we care about.

Life in the easy lane is over. We are all now in a race that has no finish line. Each person will have to be brighter, smarter, more confident and more able, both personally and professionally, to succeed in an ever-challenging, complex world.

Read this book carefully—apply the lessons thoroughly—and you will indeed help your children find the right path to a bright future. Remember, we do not owe our children a brighter future . . . But we do owe our future brighter children. You can begin with this book to ensure yours will be among the brightest . . . and the legacies you leave, the most rewarding.

Christopher J. Hegarty
Chairman Emeritus—NCFE

Introduction

There is much more to your legacy than the tangible assets, such as property and financial holdings, commonly referred to as your "estate." Indeed, its greatest worth may reside in those gifts you pass on that money simply cannot buy. The example you set with your own life—your experiences, your principles, your attitudes and work ethic—are as important to preserve as your wealth.

A common-sense education in handling money properly and profitably will continue to reward your heirs long after your departure. Such knowledge is valuable in and of itself, as well as being a means to future success. Thus, Part One of this book also devotes itself to the five major lessons of such an education: spending, saving, insuring, investing, and planning.

Parts Two and Three cover aspects of professional estate planning that are often neglected. The frank discussions presented therein confront issues of increasing importance to a long-lived, but aging, population. For instance, how can we, as descendants ourselves, best manage our own inheritance? How do we provide the best care for elderly parents? What are the best, proven procedures for bequeathing our assets—and our values—to our survivors? How do we involve them in our plans without undue fear, complications, or confusion?

Estate planning requires that we discuss death: a difficult task for many, but more pressing then ever before as issues of law, medicine, and taxation grow more complex and affect ever more families. It is never too soon to arrange for the protection of your estate and the perpetuity of your values! The book in hand was written with these objectives in mind; and, also, ultimately, to provide you and your loved ones with perhaps the most precious asset of all: peace of mind.

Kim Ciccarelli Banta
Loren Dunton

PART I

Retirement: Before & After

When my grandfathers retired they were expected to live another five years. One lived for almost 10 years, one for only two. That was many years ago. However, most people reading this book will retire at 60 or 70 or somewhere in between. Perhaps you already have. People retiring today will often live for another 20 years, and some never retire.

If you are typical, and aren't already retired, you will become an "older person"—if you're lucky, that is. You'll have problems that very few of your grandparents even thought about. But you will also have opportunities they never had. One of them is the time to become the older person you would like to be. Or at least the kind of older person your children and grandchildren would like you to be.

This is one of the legacies you will want to leave them. Part One of this book is designed to help you be the kind of older person who will leave behind memories and relationships that are positive. They can represent treasured legacies for those you care about.

Those who live this average number of years in retirement will have time for loved ones that our grandparents never had. This time, however, poses an obligation to pass on the kind of legacies I talk about in Part One.

You will be eager to read and act upon the very valuable advice Kim and her associates have for you in Part Two and Three. But remember . . . as she and I wrote in the Introduction, there is a desperate need to discuss many of the issues I talk about in Part One.

It is one of the reasons we have started the book this way.

The Three Stages
of Retirement

*"A financial mistake at 30 can be painful but a
financial mistake at 60 can be a catastrophe."*

Anyone over 50 years old has grown up in an era during which the
age brackets in this country have been categorized by the use of these
terms:

- Childhood
- Adolescence
- Youth
- Middle Age
- Old Age

In the first half of this century, these were undoubtedly the stages
which most people went through and with which they had no trouble
identifying. We live in a different world now.

Few changes are more pronounced than those pertaining to aging.
Retirement used to be almost synonymous with old age. In the 20
years after World War II, however, early and mandatory retirement
became almost universal. A recognition gradually came about that
there was a new sequence in aging: middle age, retirement, and then
old age.

In more recent years, some of us contend that retirement itself, for
more and more people, is now divided into three stages. Some of us
describe them as "active retirement," "relaxed living," and "life extension."

We firmly believe that there is much to be gained by the individual
and the professionals involved when retirement is recognized, thought
of, and planned for within the framework of these three phases. Too

many of us intimately involved with older people turn our backs on real problems and take the position that anyone who has "planned for his or her retirement" can relax and anticipate no further complications.

Active Retirement: When?

First, of course, comes the decision to retire. For this there is no pat formula or specific advice to fit everyone.

Over the years we've had many visits and interviews with retired people and those thinking of retirement.

The decision to retire is perhaps the most important and the most difficult. It plays a large role in the peace of mind we have or don't have as we live in retirement. This decision plays a large part in what legacies we leave . . . and we're not talking just about money. One conversation I remember went something like this:

"My mother was retired, bored, and so unpleasant she was driving my husband and me apart. But it's her home and while Herb was getting his doctorate, we had to put up with it."

Sound familiar?

Probably not. It isn't the type of statement we usually hear directly. Entirely too many people who are retired are as unpleasant as the mother referred to above or leave a legacy of unpleasant memories.

This woman probably retired too soon. Maybe she was just looking at her retirement in the wrong way, or maybe she needed to think more like Mary Louise Boswell of Stockton, California, whom I remember so clearly.

After a long and satisfying career as an entertainer and mother of seven children ranging in age from 30 to 50, this talented woman, some years ago, retired and moved in with her youngest daughter and son-in-law. She was a widely traveled woman of the world who could have become very unhappy in Stockton. It's a small city compared to many capitals of the world in which she entertained or traveled with her husband.

Her retirement years, as with so many, could have been filled with regrets, frustrations over getting old, and unhappiness. But they were not.

She didn't sit around and become jealous of the more exciting things the younger generation was doing. She, too, could have become as unpleasant as the mother we talked about on the previous page. Instead, she decided not only to help financially, but also to take over most of the household chores. It enabled her daughter, Virginia, to concentrate on her career and Phil, her son-in-law, to go back to school (at age 45) and get his law degree.

She "un-retired" herself.

She did something else. She made the kitchen and the dining room her new and special challenge. The applause which she heard so much during her earlier life she still heard. It came from the many dinner guests of that popular Stockton couple.

It is better to retire early, with the right attitude, than it is to retire late with the wrong attitude. One the other hand, it is better to retire late with the right attitude than to retire early with the wrong attitude.

You already know we're very much against mandatory retirement. This doesn't mean that we're not in favor of early retirement for a great many people. We have seen numbers of people, unhappy and unrewarded in their work who really only started to live after they retired. We're in favor of this.

The point is, and it is one I want to make in this chapter, even mandatory retirement laws do not determine what life in retirement will be like. The years after retirement can be truly the vintage ones. The legislators can't keep them from being that if you don't let them.

It's also important not to kid yourself. If you don't want to work any longer, admit it. Just tell people you want to retire. Don't say you are sick or too old.

What happens all too often with people who want to retire, especially if they feel defensive about it, is that they give themselves and others some cock-and-bull story about not being well. So what happens then? They gradually acquire the image and worse, the self-image, of someone who isn't well.

Pretty soon with the mind being the powerful force it is, they do get sick—sometimes years ahead of when they would have otherwise. Don't let this happen to you. If it is happening, stop it now.

Here are the five most important questions to ask yourself before you make a decision as to whether or not you should retire.

First, will my income, in retirement, be enough to give me peace of mind?

You'll notice I said nothing about how much money, if any, and in what form. This is far less important than your peace of mind. People's lifestyles after retirement, and how much money that takes to maintain, can vary so widely that any rules of thumb are meaningless, but peace of mind isn't.

Second, am I enjoying the work I am doing? If so, would I enjoy as much—whatever I would likely be doing in its place?

Some people have the knack of enjoying whatever they do. You should remember that there are probably many other things you would enjoy doing that would provide the additional life-enriching stimulation of new challenges and satisfactions. Others, of course, never enjoy anything they do. If you are one of those unfortunate souls, you should approach this same question from the negative point of view. Give some thought as to whether you might be more unhappy if you retire.

If you've never found anything you enjoy doing by the time you approach retirement age, you probably won't after retirement either.

Third, what about the significant people in my life?

This is a very important question and shouldn't be treated too casually. If you have a spouse, have you really gone into the matter carefully together? Have you been honest with yourselves? Do you know what will take the place of your work? What will fill up those long hours? How does he, or she, feel about it? There are probably others like children, neighbors, close friends, and relatives whom you should consult. Be sure you've weighed these factors. If they will play a part in your life after retirement, be sure you have taken this into account. Their input can be valuable.

Fourth, how will my lifestyle change, and what will this mean to me? To the people I care about? To the legacies I mean to leave? To the peace of mind I want?

Like the others, this is a major question which will lead to a dozen more. Ask them of yourself. Investigate. Get the facts that will help you make an intelligent decision.

Fifth, when do I want to retire?

No one who has done any research on this matter of retirement can help but be struck with the number of people who decide to retire, and just retire, sometimes with almost no thought as to when is the best time to retire. Once they've decided to retire, they want to do it, often at the earliest possible time.

This can be a real mistake.

The decision of whether or not to retire and the decision as to when to retire, should be closely tied.

One of the most interesting comments we've heard about retirement as it relates to men versus women, was made by an attractive and vibrant then-70 year old Isabel Dorst of Laguna Hills, California. With more and more women now retiring from a successful business career as she did some years ago, her comments were unusually pertinent.

"Women are less affected by their own retirement than men, but very much affected by their husband's retirement. The majority of them are climbing the walls when their spouses leave their employment. That is because, I think, women have a great many household interests even if they have been business women for years. After the men have caught up with the carpentry or gardening that they've been saving up they don't know what to do with themselves."

I asked her to tell me (in her own words) about her own retirement, and that of her husband, Louis.

"Of course, I had my plan for retiring and retired earlier than I needed to. I was very happy in my job, but I was afraid that if I waited another 10 years I would have lost the enthusiasm for attending university. That 10 years was worth a million dollars to me, for the experience of college and the other interesting things it encouraged me to do.

Louis went to real estate school before he retired, and was ready to begin another career. He left this early, too, to come to Leisure World. By the time he made this change he was really ready to devote himself to leisure pursuits. Now we both feel we wouldn't have time for business. But I've met people here who are in good health but they can't find anything they like to do. With so many things in our world of interest I find it difficult to understand their attitude, of course, and I feel that somewhere you could make the point of doing something, though it may be an effort to start.

It has taken some push this last week to get out of the house in the rain and go swimming, yet I've found that if I will do it, I always feel refreshed and interested in doing something else after. I feel that what people most miss in the first years of retirement is a schedule of some kind. Not a daily commitment, some class or meeting or just a morning or evening walk. It is quite a jolt, after having at least eight hours of one's day scheduled so that it takes little thought, except that it must be got through, to have 24 hours to be filled, each one separately."

It is tempting, of course, to go on in this chapter and list some of the many things that people can do when they retire.

Irving Heller, diamond importer and appraiser of San Francisco, once said about retirement:

"Not me, not in a million years. If you like what you're doing, why retire?"

Of course, if you have reason to think you might enjoy retirement more, it's worth considering. It could give you more time to leave legacies that will enhance your time on earth. Preserving your health and peace of mind can be as important as preserving your wealth.

2

Active Retirement
for Preserving
Your Peace of Mind

*"One good estate planning retirement
idea from a professional can be worth far
more than the fee."*

Some people contemplate retirement and too many of those already retired think of "active sports" when we talk about active retirement as a stage.

It is much more than that! It starts with replacing some of the "I can't" in our vocabulary with phrases such as "maybe I can" or " I can at least try" or "at least I could do that." We both like to say to people "who says you can't?"

You may not say "I can't" as often as kids do. But you probably think it even more often. If you're like the typical 60–90-year-olds in this country, you often say things like:

"I can't!"

"I can't get out as often as I used to."

"I can't remember names any more."

"I can't quit smoking at my age."

"I can't take up a new hobby this late in life."

"I can't seem to get around to writing letters"

"I can't start dating at my age."

"I can't change my will after this many years."

Thankfully there are many older people, however, who go right on in their 60s, 70s, and 80s, proving they *can*, instead of saying "I can't." Being one of those is a legacy worth leaving.

When we turn the spotlight on a few of them, we realize they are "just folks" like the rest of us. Celebrities? No. Special? You bet! These we can emulate!

They are ordinary people who have been unwilling to accept the idea that getting older automatically means they can't do things they want to do. One of them is Frank Judy, formerly of Baltimore. He retired as a carpenter foreman many years ago and moved to Montana at age 70. He was on the Madison River when he talked like this:

"My kids wanted us to move to Florida and bask in the sun. And we did for a while. I had always wanted to take up trout fishing though, so when my wife died, I moved to Montana."

This is the "I can" attitude! What a legacy of pride it must have been for his children.

Mr. Judy could have continued to sit on his fanny and do nothing— as he was doing in Florida. To himself, he could have said, "I can't now, I'm too old."

He didn't, though.

What he said was, "I can." And he did.

He was really making a harvest of long delayed pleasures out of his vintage years.

A lot of us admired that petite stage and movie actress, Ruth Gordon, especially when she was eighty years old. Her autobiography, *My Side*, was published and made fascinating reading—especially if you're anywhere near her age. She died leaving wonderful legacies for all of us.

Maybe you can't write a book. And you aren't a famous actress. Okay, let's put aside Ruth Gordon for now and talk about Frances Johnsen . . . "and make sure you spell that with an 'e'."

All she did was raise two families. She never held an outside job in her life. Her world centered around two husbands, seven children and twelve grandchildren. She couldn't type and didn't even like to drive a car.

She did like people, though.

When a neighbor friend told her she should go into selling, the thought scared her to death and she dismissed the idea with a laugh. The first thought that popped in her mind, she told us, was, "I can't sell."

But then she did something very smart, something we should all do more often. She asked herself, "Why can't I?"

When she couldn't come up with a good answer to the question, she went over to see her friend and talk more about becoming a saleslady.

It took her less than a year to become one of the top salesladies in her region. She sold more vitamins, food supplements, and household products than people half her age. Pretty good for a 50-year-old, wasn't it? It was even better for a 70-year-old, which she was. Of course, she had one thing going for her. She would rather figure out how she *could* than say, "I can't."

We could go on and on in this vein but you probably know enough people like this yourself—everyday people whom you admire, as would we if we knew them. You yourself may be one of them. Such people do things despite the fact that they have passed 50, 60, or 70.

We so often say nothing about the ones that really make all of us shake our heads because they go on doing things that seem hard to believe for the rest of us.

Eric de Reynier of Oakland, California, is a good example of that type; not at all typical as you will see, but more of an inspiration. He flew a hang-glider. He also continued to ride a very large motorcycle which might give you the wrong idea.

You would realize you have the wrong mental picture of Eric if you were to go through his beautiful home filled with antique furniture and *objets d'art* from three continents. When you meet him you aren't surprised that this handsome silverhaired gentleman with a delightful accent is a connoisseur of Chinese art.

What one is surprised at is that when he was almost 74 years old, he spent most weekends flying around and hanging from the same type of Delta wing that the 20- and 30-year-olds were flying.

Should you quit saying "I can't" and go out and take up some dangerous sport such as this? Of course not.

A great many people need to quit spending so much time thinking of things they can't do and spend more time thinking of things that other people do do.

Read Alex Comfort's terrific book *A Good Age*. It is still one of the best books on the subject.

But don't turn to it for inspiration or motivation. You may read about Victor Hugo and his writing accomplishments at 81 and mentally shake your head at his greatness, but not identify. You may know you could never write like that, especially at your age.

But who says you have to?

Why do you even have to be published?

Put down the book and look around. You might see a number of your contemporaries finding great satisfaction just writing letters.

Let us tell you about Effie Corum Pelton. She was a pioneer lady, mother, grandmother, great grandmother before she died. Self-educated and hard of hearing, she taught herself to type late in life and practiced with long, newsy but fun letters to her children and grandchildren.

Then she graduated to writing to newspaper columnists and editors in Sacramento. It was when she was almost 80 years old that they found out she was right about turkeys, a certain kind of turkey. She got quoted . . . and in her family, neighborhood, and Queens Club she was applauded.

She moved to Montana when she was 80 and did the same thing. Those newspaper columns with her name in them were just a few of the fun legacies she left to her children.

You might find it in a little theater group across town. You may also be surprised how many amateur, fun plays are performed by groups composed entirely of retired people.

Isabel Dorst, whom her friends called Mimi, had never done any acting until she was almost 70. She never did appear on Broadway, but how much fun she and her friends in that Leisure World retirement community had putting on plays for neighbors and friends.

If you really want to be impressed (and intimidated), read *A Good Age* about Arthur Rubinstein. He was a tremendous man and talented. But if you want to do something you can talk to a music teacher about taking lessons. Look forward to playing for the family. Look forward to learning to play the piano for its own sake, for your sake.

Why let the fact that you're never going to play at Carnegie Hall keep you from learning to play the piano? Just playing is still a legacy worth leaving.

Have you ever sewed? Or do you sew?

You might want to quit sewing when you read about Coco Chanel's triumphant return to the fashion world at age 71. Don't. Put the book down, get dressed up a little bit, and go down to the local sewing center or go see some friend who sews.

Have some fun designing something. What does it really matter to your mirror if it doesn't equal Coco's designs? Think of the satisfaction. And it can impress grandchildren.

It is tempting to go on and on.

But you get the idea.

A Different Kind of "I Can't"

The discussion that was going on really had to do with retirement but a friend of mine, an astute observer of the social scene, made an interesting observation about the difference between older men and older women.

"Women at 65 are still needed," he said, "while most men's usefulness is all over."

His wife suggested that this might very well have a lot to do with the difference in the longevity of men and women.

"Maybe being needed, or continuing to be needed, has more to do with staying alive than most people think."

One day a 66-year-old neighbor complained about the fact that "they don't need us old duffers anymore." He was talking about the company with which he had been associated for over 30 years. It was obvious as one listened to him that what he was really saying was:

"I can't find anything to do, because nobody needs me."

Here was a man who had headed up an accounting department that at one time employed 60 people. He was used to solving problems and figuring out ways to do things if those working for him couldn't find the answers. Now he was retired and it seemed that every bit of the resourcefulness that had made him a good executive had deserted him. More accurately, he had deserted it and put "I can't" in its place.

He had turned from an "I can" man of 64 into an "I can't" man of 65. Isn't that ridiculous?

Think about it. Here was a man with a probable life expectancy of 10 to 20 years, with a valuable background of experience he wasn't even putting to work for an even more important cause than his company.

His own future.

He didn't need money. He did need not to have his talents and experience turn into a useless commodity. Which they weren't. They were valuable. But instead of trying to find where they might be put to work, where he might be needed, he spent his time complaining about his old company and the young "amateurs" who were now in his place.

What might he have done?

One man with a similar background checked with his Chamber of

Commerce and found out about the SCORE program for retired executives. It gave him a whole new lease on life.

Get busy and find out. It's your life that's at stake. Maybe not your life, if you want to quibble, but certainly your happiness. Start making some phone calls. Start asking around. That's what we all need to do.

One man we know is absolutely fuming about the sad state of the financial affairs of a very large volunteer organization whose name we won't mention, although the bookkeeping he was upset about was just that of the local chapter.

He may still be fuming, but he is also having a ball straightening the books out and undoubtedly enjoying the expressions of amazement and appreciation coming from the delightful ladies with whom it brings him in contact. Do you think that is the only non-profit organization that needs help?

Just don't say "I can't."

At least unless you've given it (whatever it is) a real try.

The point we want to make here is that too many older people complain but think to themselves, "I can't do anything about it," before they've even tried.

We don't want to belabor the point, but we would like to suggest something else to say once in a while.

"Who the hell says I can't?"

The memory of you saying something like this occasionally is a wonderful legacy to leave. If you want to prove something to your heirs get involved in Mary Furlong's SENIOR NET of San Francisco "Computer fun for seniors." It's all over the country.

3

Your Attitude: All-Important for the Same Reason

"The choosing of a financial advisor is more important than choosing an insurance company or securities products."

For those of you interested in leaving a legacy of positive memories, you need to develop in all three stages of retirement the type of positive and loving attitude that you want to be remembered as having.

One of the things that too few people, men and women, fail to take into account about the very important trait of attitude is that it becomes more important as one gets older. When you're younger, you can make up for a poor attitude, at least partially, by doing one or more of several things. You can work harder, for example, put in more hours. Or you can work smarter, become more educated in what you have to do.

Happiness, to a large extent, has been dependent on the success you are having in your work. Recognition played an important part—a growing bank account, a more impressive home and car. Yet these are all external factors, outside things, all of them.

The world has changed.

Happiness and peace of mind, more and more, come from within if they come at all. Accomplishments play a far less important role. You are now the focus. The kind of person you are. The way other people, friends, relatives, and even strangers react to *you*.

Fortunately, the factor that determines happiness, more than your apparent status in life, is your own attitude about life. If it isn't good,

15

you can change it. It may not be easy, but it will always be to your great benefit.

If you have a bad attitude, about retirement, getting older, or about some of the infirmities that seem to go hand-in-hand with the aging process, then you need to get rid of it. Don't wait. Start to work on it right now. You need to have a good attitude about yourself to make the right decisions about your estate.

Attitudes show up in a dozen ways every day when you're: critical of the least little thing; make a big issue out of the slightest discomfort or inconvenience; react negatively to suggestions made to you, even when you acknowledge that they are for your own good; look only upon the bad side of every incident; only grunt when you're spoken to; smile so seldom that it hurts your face when you do; never smile first, of course; and you complain.

You probably know also the price you pay for having an unpleasant attitude. Your relationship with your spouse isn't nearly as rewarding as it could be, friends who could do a great deal to reduce the amount of loneliness you feel avoid you instead of seeking out your company. Relatives, especially children and grandchildren, limit their contact except as a duty, and you sense it. New acquaintances don't warm up to you and you miss the opportunity to make new friends. These are not good legacies to leave!

We could go on and on. We know the price we pay when we have a bad attitude. You know too, in your heart, that people with a good attitude toward life and getting older are a lot happier. Instead of paying prices like those above, they receive the dividend of better relationships, of more friends, of more options as to what to do with their time and of more pleasant human contacts.

Why dwell any more on the difference?

Instead we have some suggestions for getting rid of a bad attitude. First, forget about getting rid of it. A bad attitude is like a bad habit more than anything else; you don't break a bad habit by trying to get rid of it.

Here's How to Do It

What happens, and you all know this, when you try to break a bad habit? You're left with a vacuum. A vacuum, of course, works to fill itself. In this case, usually, with a variation of the same old bad habit. To change a habit pattern, or to change your attitude, you need to replace the bad one you have with a better one. To effect any real change in yourself, you need to replace the bad habit of being negative with the habit of being positive.

This means that what we have to talk about is how to acquire a good attitude toward retirement and getting older. We have to talk about *how* to replace the bad attitude if we admit we have one. To this end, we present a five-step formula.

1. Admit That Your Attitude Is Bad. If you've already done this, you're over an important hurdle and have a big advantage over a large percentage of the senior citizen population right now.

2. Review the Benefits. At least in your mind, review the last few pages about the importance of having a good attitude, especially the dividends that might come to you personally from having a better one. Everybody needs incentives. You need to give yourself as many incentives as you can think of.

3. Use the Mirror Technique in the Morning. The very first time you look in the mirror, pause a moment. Look yourself in the eye and smile. Sure, it's an important task to assign yourself, with some tremendous benefits, but a little smile, even a laugh at ourselves, can be a good thing. Besides, for some of you getting back the smile you haven't had for years is an absolute necessity if you're really going to develop a better attitude about the rest of your life.

4. Use the Power of Your Subconscious. One of the best ways to harness this power is to learn to condition your mind at the right time. When you're trying to effect a change, that is. The best time is just before you fall asleep. The conscious mind is less distracted and more receptive. The main thing, however, is that it is the best time to get a message into your subconscious. So review the day but don't dwell on the failures. Instead, concentrate on remembering the times when your attitude seemed better than at other times. Perhaps when you were friendlier. You need to get that picture in your mind of being a more positive, friendlier person with a better attitude. Try to hold that mental picture as you fall asleep.

5. Use a Reminder. Put some small thing in your pocket or purse, something you'll feel or see several times a day, something you haven't been carrying before. It could be a special coin. Even a small rock or a three-by-five card. Give it some thought. You want it to serve as a reminder. We all need reminders and it should serve that purpose. When you feel it or see it, it should bring to mind the fact that you have embarked on a campaign to quit feeling sorry for yourself and have a better attitude about getting old. At least we hope we will, get old, that is.

The alternative gives you no choice.

One last word about a project like this, a self-improvement program, if you will. For some reason, older people so often feel that self-improvement is only for the young. Not so. Self-improvement is for anyone who has the time and something to gain by improving. You see there is much to gain when you realize that the memories of those with whom you come in contact are part of the legacy you leave behind. Make an effort to see that a positive attitude, or at least the memory of your own positive attitude, is one of the legacies you pass on to those you care about.

4

Aging, Learning, and Staying Well

"Bad decisions are most often made without proper knowledge."

Have you wanted to know the origin of this ridiculous idea that people over 50 have difficulty learning new things? We know it's ridiculous because millions of people over 50, 60, 70, and 80 have proven it wrong by their own learning accomplishments. Here are three places where this idea originates, but there are more.

First: Younger employees in thousands of companies across the country, for generations, have had something to gain by promoting the myth that older people in the job hierarchy were getting a little slow to learn new things.

"You know, the boss doesn't pick up things quite as fast as he used to." Or, "Old Fred, who heads up my department, has really slowed down."

Of course, young Bob who wants the job won't come right out and say anything specific, but the damage has been done. Older Fred doesn't usually get a chance to defend his slowness in taking to new ideas. He doesn't get a chance very often to explain that sometimes this apparent slowness to grasp and run with a new idea isn't due to any lessened learning ability, but rather the wisdom and caution he has acquired with age and experience. There are many variations on this theme in companies and organizations around the country. We could list dozens of examples that strike close to home for all of us over 50.

The point is that there are reasons why the myth is continually fed.

However, it doesn't only originate in the work forces. Those of you in your 50s, 60s, and 70s see it in your families, too. Maybe your children aren't guilty of saying anything like this, and if they are, it's probably for your own good. At least they think it is.

"Why don't you let me do that, Mom? You know you don't see as well as you once did."

"Why worry about having to manage that big place all by yourself? Why don't you sell it and come live with us?"

"You know, Dad, these new government regulations are pretty tricky to keep up with and you don't really have the time."

You want to know an interesting story about that last quote? It has to do with the father who was telling about an organization he founded. He wasn't even resentful, only amused, at how his two sons took over the business. This is about the way he told the story. "It started with a new set of forms that the agency wanted a firm like ours to fill out quarterly. I was still head of the company and doing a pretty damn good job going by the bottom line on our annual statement. But the boys were eager to take over, which was okay. They apparently felt, however, that they had to make me question my own ability before they could do much about taking over."

According to the sharp older gentleman telling the story, questioning his ability took many forms and he actually did lose some confidence in his ability to keep up with the new business climate. His company had to cooperate, but listen to what happened.

"The new regulations which they felt were too complicated for me and finally precipitated the discussion that lead to my getting out, never were handled by my sons. They also found the regulations too complicated and brought in an outside accounting firm which would have been a sign of approaching senility had I done it."

He laughed when he told the story. In his case they were doing him a favor. He now has had almost 20 years of living it up and having more fun in retirement than he did the last five years in his business because of the government bureaucracy.

But what about other examples? Some of them aren't funny. There have been situations in which older people were made to feel mentally inadequate so that sons and daughters (often well meaning ones) could take over. Maybe the home, maybe the business, maybe just taking over their decision making. Or perhaps just talking down to them.

They all feed the myth that getting older is always the explanation. This myth is often the explanation for the "role-reversal" that regularly takes place between older parents and adult children. They rationalize it, of course.

"Dad's now 61 and not quite as sharp as he used to be."

"Mother doesn't think as straight as she used to."

When a younger persons fails, it might be because he or she had a hangover or didn't do enough research, or had his or her mind on something else, or was being harassed by the kids. There are a thousand valid reasons for flubbing something without losing face. We think nothing about it except when it's people in their 60s or 70s and then "getting older" is automatically the explanation. It's all part of the myth, of course.

Let's get to the third reason why the myth that older people can't learn continues. Too many of us stop trying to learn. It's that simple. Some older people haven't tried to learn anything new since they retired. Some people who are planning to retire soon should be looking forward to all the time they now have for learning. Unfortunately, most people in that category haven't even taken the time to learn about retirement itself. We perpetuate the myth by proving it true.

Take Another Look At Learning

"Aging itself is not automatically detrimental to learning ability and I.Q. It is time to reassess the view that learning depends on age."

Psychologist Richard L. Sprott, who was involved in the study of genetics in the Jackson Laboratory in Bar Harbour, Maine, said this when he was speaking to about 60 scientists from throughout the United States. He went on to say, "The factor involved in learning is the health of the individual growing older."

This was the third time in one year that newspapers had carried stories to this effect.

"We have 22 residents over 70 years of age signed up for college credit courses being put on by the De Anza College." This was the manager of the Retirement Inn of Sunnyvale, California speaking. What a nice legacy for those people to leave.

Now in the 1990s learning for seniors is a well-accepted thing but even in 1980, when learning for seniors was starting to take off, she also said, "Furthermore, some of the older people in the class not only are the most eager, but seem to be doing the best job of learning." It didn't take very much research on my part to confirm what my own experience had taught me. People's ability to learn and their eagerness to do so has very little relationship to their age, but a much greater relationship to their health.

There is something else, however, that might be even more responsible for those elders who do keep on learning all their lives. Actually, it is a key factor in the difference between them and those who have slowed down a lot—one word: *Attitude.* Some people are stuck in front of the television and don't even know where the library is. They probably haven't enrolled in a class in 20 years. They haven't become interested in a new subject for so long they feel they don't even have anything interesting to talk about . . . and they don't have.

Furthermore, these people are probably not spending enough time around people who do have something worth talking about, so that it rubs off on them. Naturally, they feel they bore those around them. They probably do, but it's not because of their age. It might be because they've stopped learning anything new, and why have they done that? Partly, or at least in some cases, it's because they've become lazy. But in a lot of other cases, it's because they've accepted that myth about the loss of learning power. So what do you do about it? Yes, we do have some suggestions about what to learn. But first and foremost, work on your *attitude.* It might even be worthwhile to go back and review Chapter 3. As far as your attitude about learning, we remind you first that a lot of younger people can't learn things as quickly as they would like to, either. Age isn't always to blame.

Second, older people need to pay a little more attention to the scientists and other authorities who are now, especially in the 90s, refuting the myth about aging and learning. Pay less attention to those around you who foster the myth. You need more positive input to counteract all the negatives you are exposed to daily.

Third, become more selective about people with whom you spend your time. Associate more with those who are still interested in things, who are still learning. Cultivate those associations because they play a tremendous role in the way you think and the way your attitudes are formed and modified.

Finally, if you really want to have a better attitude about yourself, and that's what it gets down to, of course, watch what you tell yourself. Make a conscious effort to disprove the idea that you've lost your ability to learn. Consciously think more about the things you have learned and are learning.

Few legacies can you leave that will have more far-reaching effects for your loved ones who come after you than to say things like, "You know, my XYZ had a wonderful attitude right up until the day he or she went into the hospital."

Staying Well Emotionally

We have stressed attitudes and ways of thinking because authorities are now so much in agreement that the way we think and what we feed into our subconscious plays such a large part in our health and happiness; ones that can help us stay well and age more slowly.

"My circulation is so bad I don't enjoy sitting watching television like I used to."

Believe it or not, the man saying this was not even 70, and had been retired three years. Despite this, this man was continuing to ignore his doctor's advice about getting out and walking. Yes, despite repeated warnings from his doctor and the misguided nagging from his daughter, this man "had given up" to such an extent that he wouldn't even take walks with his wife and enjoy the ocean they live near.

What we do know for sure is the amount of effort, time, and physical well-being put into exercise and having a good attitude probably pays more dividends than anything else we can think of. Are you a little skeptical of the power that the mind has to keep one well; to delay the aging process? Do you tend to think that the germs, viruses, plus the ravages of time are omnipotent?

Norman Cousins, the highly respected former editor of *The Saturday Review* described in *The New England Journal of Medicine* way back in December, 1976, how he laughed his way out of a crippling disease that doctors thought incurable. He said then and has been quoted many times in the years since, "I have learned never to underestimate the capacity of the human mind and body to regenerate—even when the prospects seem most wretched."

Surely if a respected thinker and realist such as Norman Cousins could say things about this capacity to regenerate and prove it in his own life, it should be easy for the rest of us to accept the idea that "staying well" is relatively easy if the mind and the body are working together. He said something else impressive all those years ago. "I made the joyous discovery that 10 minutes of genuine belly laughter had an anesthetic effect and would give me at least two hours of pain-free sleep."

He went on to tell in a later book about how laughter and "positive emotions" affected his body chemistry for the better. "I was greatly elated by the discovery that there is a psychological basis for the ancient theory that "laughter is good medicine." Thought-provoking, isn't it?

A few extra years of staying well and healthy is a wonderful legacy to leave to those you care about. The peace of mind it can give you as you plan your estate is priceless.

5

Getting Along with Kids and Grandkids

"Developing a long-term relationship with your financial professional is as helpful as keeping the same doctors."

Ann Linning Smith, seminar leader at Piedmont Gardens in Piedmont, California said several years ago, "There are a lot of residents living here whose families either live in Timbuktu, or pretend they do." Older people are so often ignored by their adult children and grandchildren. In recent years we see how prevalent this is.

Families could afford to visit often, but they are just too busy. Part of the reason some families stay away, however, is the fault of the older people who live there. Would you like to know why?

Guilt

If so, listen to this quote taken almost verbatim as a visitor was leaving one beautiful senior complex. "We would visit more often if it wasn't so hard to get away. Our parents make us feel guilty for leaving so soon. Invariably, we are late to wherever else we are going."

Can you see the disservice older folks do to themselves when they cause relatives to think that they don't dare visit if they only have a few minutes? It doesn't matter where you live. For many people the problem starts long before they move into a retirement community. Sure, you might like to visit at greater length. Sure, you have things to tell and things you would like to hear about the family, but making people feel guilty is the best way to cut down on the number of visits you receive.

There are two ways that most older people react when the visitor is getting ready to leave. Most often they actually complain. They say something to the effect, "Do you really have to leave so soon?", but not as a polite and indirect way of saying how much they are enjoying having them there. Oh no, they say it almost invariably in a whiny, complaining voice.

A mother finally was told off by her son-in-law when she was guilty of this once too often. "Mom," he told her, "You tell about how Arnold (the other son-in-law) and Helen always stay a couple of hours when they come to visit you, but you forget that Jane and I stay a couple of hours sometimes, too. What we also do, however, that Arnold and Helen don't do, is drop in when we have only 20 minutes. Arnold and Helen just drive on by when they don't have a couple of hours."

He let her think about this for a moment. Then he said, "If you would be happier if we only came by when we have a couple of hours to visit, we will just cut out the short visits."

She saw what she was doing and got back her perspective. She admitted how much she would miss the short visits.

Do you see what a mistake it is to make children (or grandchildren) sorry they stopped by for a moment? Isn't this one of the legacies you want to leave them? These short, happy visits they had with you where you expressed joy instead of disappointment?

How much better it is to say how glad you are that they came. What you should want to accomplish is to get them to come back soon. The basic rule to bring this about is to make them glad they came.

Ann Smith, who made the opening remark about relatives who live in Timbuktu, said something else very much worth noting. Those of you who are grandparents should listen carefully to her words, "I had both my grandmothers living with me when I was a child. One of them was a real bitch."

Did old age make her so difficult, she was asked.

"No, she had been difficult ever since mother and dad were married, maybe even before."

This kind of statement suggests there are a lot of older people in society today who don't seem to realize that their grandchildren become thoughtful, aware human beings at a very early age. Some might think they are fooling their grandchildren, but if they have been unpleasant to the grandchildren's mommy and daddy, it won't be forgotten. Grandchildren might like you because you bring them toys and candy and a dollar once in a while, but you will be remembered for the kind of person you were to their parents, as well as for the things you did for them.

It is one of the legacies you will leave them. Decide whether it will be a positive or negative one.

Your Personal Legacy: Three Questions to Ask Yourself

We have other ideas about the way people should or should not relate to younger members of a family, whether it's the second, third, or fourth generation. These are ways to relate, that is, if you want to leave a legacy of good feelings that will enrich their lives.

To start out, answer these three questions:

1. Do you feel that because you are older you don't need to practice the basic rules of good human relations, or even common courtesy?
2. Why are you polite and wonderful with other people and often rude and discourteous with your children and grandchildren?
3. Why do you apparently resent being discriminated against just because you are older yet expect to be liked and treated royally because of your age?

Let's discuss these one by one.

If you don't care about being liked or loved, then courtesy and the basic principles of good human relations are things you can ignore; but that doesn't apply to everyone. Some people don't have many friends. They are bored, have nothing to do, and no one to do it with.

Practicing good, common courtesy will pay dividends no matter how old you are, whether you are in your 40s, 50s, 60s, 70s or 80s. At the end of the chapter is a list of 10 rules for good human relations. These rules seem most important for those of you who want to leave other legacies besides money and property.

Are you really entitled to extra benefits from life and from other people just because you might be older?

We don't think so.

"Don't you believe in helping little old ladies across the street?"

Of course. You'd probably help a young person with a white cane too; but that has nothing to do with age. If you help people, it is because they're frail, have a disability, or may appreciate the gesture. It should not be just because they're old.

The same principle applies to the basic rules of good human relations we referred to in question number two. You have no right to ignore sound principles and common courtesies with your kids and grandkids just because you are older. "But they will love me anyway," isn't something you should let yourself think.

Perhaps they will, of course, love you anyway. But will they do the nice things for you that they would otherwise? Will they come to visit you as often when you are a lot older and eating your heart out for their company? Trading on one's age is not something that will endear you to those you care about.

It is logical, of course, to expect some differences because of your greater years; but, it isn't logical if you are unwilling to assume whatever obligations might come with those years.

It's worth a thought.

The Importance of a Response

"I wrote grandma all about it, but I never heard from her."

That was a little girl talking. It can remind all of us of something we find too easy to forget.

When people don't write many letters, the ones they do write assume an unusual importance. They expect an answer, even if the letter itself doesn't call for one. In the little girl's case, it was very important to her to know not that she had told grandma, but that grandma had read what she had told her. If we want to be popular with our grandkids, we need to remember the acknowledgement.

Sometimes you don't have time to write a letter. Send a note, just an acknowledgement, but right away. Then if we never get around to writing a letter, they will at least have that note. We will not have lost important ground with some grandchild that we can lose by ignoring the letter.

At Least Interest If Not Involvement

One of the real secrets of seeming younger than we are, and being popular with our kids and grandkids is: keeping our *interest*. All you should lose is your involvement.

So it's worth telling yourself "stay interested."

The Ten Rules I Promised You

They really come from Charles B. Roth, psychologist and motivator, who died some years ago after a lifetime of working in sales and the self-improvement areas. As he approached his 70s, he often was frustrated by the tendency older people have to quit practicing good human relations. These are the 10 points he rated so highly:

1. Love . . . you give it.
2. Understanding . . . you search for it.
3. Friendliness . . . you feel it.
4. Concern . . . you express it.
5. Generosity . . . you invest it.
6. Talk . . . you do it less.
7. Names . . . you use them.
8. Courtesy . . . you practice it.
9. Appreciation . . . you show it.
10. Questions . . . you ask them.

If you practice these in your 50s, 60s, 70s and 80s, the other legacies you leave—or don't leave—will be far less important. You will have left memories that will be rich legacies.

Practicing these rules can also go a long way toward preserving your peace of mind!

6

Attitudes about Sex
and Money

*"We feel that most clients need only to be
presented with the proper facts in order to
make good decisions."*

"How do you rate the valuable lessons you were given by your
parents?"

I phrased this question to a young couple who had agreed to be
interviewed. They were among those who had nothing but good things
to say about their parents.

The time of this interview was well into the 1990s, and these Baby
Boomers intrigued me. How had living through the 1960s and 1970s
changed the way they looked back on the way they perceived their
upbringing. What important legacies had their parents left them?

One said money, the other said sex. They each elaborated on the
value they placed upon these two aspects of life. A healthy attitude
toward sex and knowledge of personal finance had each been transmit-
ted to them as children, and were equally valuable legacies. Their
parents genuinely loved each other and this love and mutual respect
was communicated in many ways on a daily basis. This communication of their love established a healthy, positive attitude about sex that
this young couple will be able to pass on to their own children.

It's the Attitude

Some 200 older adults live in the Notre Dame Apartments in San
Francisco, an apartment house for seniors with communal dining
facilities and recreation rooms. Their popular social worker, Betsy

Conrad, once offered to set up a meeting and follow-up interviews with a select group of five women, aged between 65 and 70.

The message that came through loud and clear during this very special interview was that we all have an obligation as we get older to be aware of what things have shaped our own attitudes...and to make allowances for them. Especially in those matters that have to do with our sex lives.

As one member of the group commented, "If older people haven't had a good sex life while they were young, they don't miss it when they get older. But if they did have, they do. Unfortunately, their attitudes and personality can be warped because of what they've missed."

"Have we so dehumanized our impassioned elders in this society that they are expected to deny their sex drives?"

This was Betsy Conrad's question. Now let me ask my own.

If a healthy attitude about sex was not one of the legacies left to you, are you at least keeping a healthy attitude yourself . . . so it can be one of the good legacies you leave?

Sex and Health

One of the people interviewed by myself and Nancy Dorst, was Albert Z. Freedman of New York, at that time editor of *Forum, the International Journal of Human Relations.* This is a large circulation magazine, sexually oriented, that features a great many letters from people all over the world telling or asking about their sex lives. *Forum's* collection of hundreds of thousands of letters is acknowledged to be the most impressive dialogue dealing with sexual behavior ever assembled.

Here is part of what Mr. Freedman had to say about sex for older people:

> All of our experience and the thousands of letters we receive, many of them from older men and women, have convinced us at *Forum* that those who attach more importance to sex after 50 or 60 or 70, instead of less importance to it, are not only happier, they are a lot healthier.

He went on to make a flat statement that their magazine could document from studies that an actual correlation exists between the cessation of sexual activity and a subsequent onset of senility.

Furthermore, there is no question that sexually liberated senior citizens who remain most active sexually are the ones least susceptible to becoming senile as they get older.

The bulk of the correspondence we have received over the last 10 years from people over 60 has definitely shown there is a very deep correlation between good health, a sense of humor, good nutrition, and pleasurable sexual activity. All of these characteristics are very important and one indeed relies on the other.

When we asked about energy levels, he replied,

. . . We have discovered that nutrition for the aged is even more important than with younger people if they are to have the energy to involve themselves sexually with a partner. Sexual activity, according to most of our writers over 60, is vital in keeping young both in mind and body. *Forum* carried original research by Dr. Paul Tabori, whom we sent to a nursing home in Vienna, Austria. We were informed that doctors had been conducting research on the link-up between sexual behavior and aging. Dr. Tabori interviewed the doctors and the people living there and experienced an atmosphere in this nursing home unlike any he had ever seen.

The doctors and the patients told him that as a result of . . . sexual relationships between the patients living there the illness rate was cut drastically. The patients started looking better, their hair quit greying and in some cases started getting darker, their skin softened, and they got a vital look back in their eyes. The rate of senility was cut sharply and a unique friendly feeling pervaded the place.

They found that "touch" for the aged is very important. That just touching even without sex was better than any medication.

We asked Dr. Freedman if the sexually liberated atmosphere had created any problems. "The only problems created came from the children of the aged residents. The fact that their parents were sexual beings was offensive to many of the adult children."

He expressed the same amazement I have always felt over this attitude and then went on.

Here was the best medicine, under doctors' supervision, and with no toxic effect. It can only help the blood circulation and improve the heart beat. It was good exercise and gave a feeling of pleasure when there was no other pleasure in their lives—all in all it was a revelation to these patients. The study confirmed what the literally hundreds of letters we have received over the past decade indicate. People in their 60s and 70s not only are capable of sexual satisfaction but are enjoying having sex. Furthermore, they believe that it keeps them young!"

Sexual Attitude Restructuring (SAR)

In researching my books, Nancy Dorst and I talked to as wide a group of interested and knowledgeable people as we could. Our questions, like the people we interviewed, ranged over a wide variety of occupations. Naturally, Nancy and I weren't surprised that Mr. Freedman would recommend an active sex life for older people, but we were at least a little surprised to find ministers so open and candid about recommending sexual activity for older married couples as a boon to both mental and physical health.

Some of these ministers are now enrolled in the Sexual Attitude Restructuring (SAR) Program put on by the National Sex Forum in San Francisco, or at the Institute for Advanced Study of Human Sexuality. Although a new institution, it is already offering four graduate degree programs with a faculty, both in residence and at large, that reads like the who's who of sexual academia.

Some years ago, Nancy Dorst and I also set up an interview with Phyllis Lyon, D.A. She was registrar of the Institute and, among other impressive credentials, is a commissioner on the San Francisco Human Rights Commission.

"One should keep in mind that the field of human sexuality has emerged as a professional discipline in only the last 10 years," she said, seemingly as a way of explaining our society's backwardness in studying this vital human activity. "If your book helps older people realize that they themselves don't need to be backward about showing an interest in their own sexuality, it will be doing them an important service."

She also made the same point that others had, about not hesitating to get therapy for sexual problems any more than one would hesitate about seeking therapy for any other problems.

"It is a shame," she said, "when older people who have earned the right to all the enjoyment and therapeutic benefits from sex that they are capable of, are reluctant to seek help."

Don't be turned off to the pleasures of sex just because you're getting older. Nor should you be turned off to the pleasures of hiking, or gardening, or playing golf, or any other healthful physical activity, just because you're getting older.

If you have enjoyed these and other activities, and there is no good reason not to continue, then continue! Don't let the attitude of others or any old myths keep you from activities, including sex, which are a natural part of life.

I suggest that you be willing to allocate more time for all enjoyable activities, especially if they boost your energy levels and promote a healthy, positive attitude.

Aaron L. Rutledge was director of the Grosse Pointe Psychological Clinic. You might be interested in his answer when asked if it would be dangerous to their health for a 60-year-old youthful couple, recently married, to have sex every night as they had been doing. "Obviously the two of you are making good use of your time and energies. Frequency does not damage sex organs, nor does it interfere with health in any way."

He then went on to say something we think is more important than any other advice he could have given. I am quoting him exactly.

"By talking freely about sexual needs, preferences and the meaning of shared experiences, a couple keeps in touch with one another."

Something else it does: it creates a valuable legacy to pass on. An example for which those you care about will someday be grateful.

Attitudes About Money

It might be too late for the average reader of this book to benefit very much from the rest of this chapter. But the younger people who you might want to help, really need advice about *spending,* or at least some of them do.

More sophisticated aspects of personal finance will be discussed in Part II of this book.

We have a technique that has helped thousands of people. We call it . . .

Spending by Choice

We want to talk about a spending technique that will help protect you from high-pressure salesmanship. The technique offers many benefits. Here is an example.

Suppose you have just been subjected to a very convincing sales demonstration of a new vacuum cleaner (or something of the sort). Very probably, the salesperson is pressing for the order since it is the nature of the job—we don't blame him or her for that. Of course, we grant salespeople the right to use sound sales psychology.

In turn, we suggest that you use sound *buying* psychology: in this case, "spending by choice" instead of buying from pressure.

Of course you want the vacuum cleaner. It is the salesperson's job to make you want it, to make it more valuable to you than the amount of money it actually takes to buy it.

May as well admit it.

But take one more step before you actually go ahead and make the purchase. Go over in your own mind the other things you might want and could buy with that same amount of money. You may be able to do it right then, or you may want to take a day to think of those other things.

Five minutes of thinking about the "choices" you have can be more valuable to you than taking all day to "think it over" and merely thinking about whether to buy it or not.

In effect, using the salesperson's system, you are "choosing *what* to buy" rather than deciding whether to buy something. This in turn leads to the *weighing of benefits* and helps you remain objective in your buying and selective in your spending. It works whether you're spending 10 cents, 10 dollars, or a 100 dollars.

Saving: Be Aware of Inflation

Over the last few years you have seen the dollar shrink to less than half of its former purchasing power. Naturally, you wonder what is going to happen in the next few years. Does the old penny postcard now really cost *that* much? Will inflation continue at the same rate we're living with now?

It's hard to believe, isn't it?

Yet who would have believed 50 years ago that the penny postcard in 1968 would go to 5¢? Or that in 1977 it would be 9¢? Or that in 1991 it would go to 15¢? Imagine what it will be in 2001.

Of course, older people are reminded of this trend much more often than others. They are reminded every time they buy a pound of butter or a dozen eggs that at one time it cost only a few pennies. They are reminded every time they write out the automobile payment, the rent check, or the house payment. The rent alone is probably more money than the breadwinner in the family was making just 30 or 40 years ago.

If you are old enough, you may have had even more painful reminders. You could not be living on the $200 or $300 a month that 40 years ago seemed like a substantial sum for retirement. Obviously, you're aware of it! Individuals or couples who do not plan ahead are certain to face many trials. But there are ways to prepare.

What to Do about It?

How can one guard against the many disappointments that are certain to be faced by the individual or the couple that does not plan ahead?

We recommend that you analyze the possible avenues for saving that have not kept up with inflation. For example, government savings bonds, bank savings accounts, or even the less generous savings and loan accounts and poorly planned life insurance savings plans at one time didn't. Now, some do.

"You mean you don't believe in these options?"

This question has been asked often in discussion sessions at investment seminars. Of course, we believe in some of them. We believe in putting money in the bank. As a matter of fact, that is the proper place for the first money over and above what you need for your day-to-day spending. And there should be enough to take care of the sudden emergencies that often arise. Few legacies you can leave will be more important than this one.

You will read more detailed approaches to personal finance in Part II and Part III of this book. Some of these can also help the younger people in your life to get an early start preserving their own wealth and peace of mind.

7

Who Is Your Legacy Going To?

"Most financial problems can be solved as long as you aren't just looking for a quick fix."

It was Alexander Pope in his essay on Man who wrote "The proper study of mankind is Man." It is still good advice today. Many of you have lived in a real-life laboratory for the study of other people all your lives. When you observe the attitudes of young people, however, you are often shocked. Perhaps more than anything else you're shocked at their obviousness. The next step is amusement and then amazement at how often the private shield young people set up between themselves and the world becomes transparent. How easy it is to see through.

An easy mistake older people make is forgetting that the young are looking at them, and that shields are often transparent. The answer lies not in a better shield against the young, but an inner view that you are not ashamed to have seen. You achieve this in part as you improve your attitude about and toward younger people. We talked about attitude before, but it's worth dwelling on for a moment now. It will play a large part in the type of personal legacy you leave.

If you are critical instead of tolerant, your expression shows it. If you develop a love for young people and a warmth with tolerance, it too is projected. Unforgotten also, is hate and intolerance. Young people feel it perhaps even more quickly. Young people in the 90s are not the radicals that many were in the 60s. What they are, that you must keep in mind, is perceptive and aware. They are also discriminating. They aren't going to like you just because you are older. You have to earn their affection with more than years.

"We would need less tolerance if we had more of something else," said a fellow dinner guest one time. The other seven were all over 70.

"What else?" asked someone at the table, curious.

"Tolerance," he said, "is a fine virtue. It's one we all need to practice. However, if we have the right attitude toward young people, we develop something better."

He went on to explain that the older person with a truly open heart develops *understanding* towards young people. He digressed for a minute and made a point of the fact that he was talking about an open heart and not a soft heart.

"Understanding," he added, "just doesn't come to us when we have a negative attitude toward young people."

The dinner broke up. We were left with two thoughts. One: that an open heart or the right attitude toward young people could bring about better understanding. Two: how much better understanding might be than tolerance.

An Interesting Project

How does one go about developing a greater understanding of how young people of today think?

Twenty years ago friend and mentor Charles B. Roth, at 70, seemed to have this ability to understand, developed to a very high degree. When asked about it he offered a simple formula to develop it. Every year since then, things have happened which proved how right his suggestion was.

"Listen when a younger person talks."

How often do you really listen? Actively listen to young people, that is? If you do, you realize, unless you're unusually modest, how it sets you apart. Makes us special, makes you someone young people like to talk to. Sometimes, however, older people become a little rusty and get careless.

If this applies to you, don't feel too badly, that is, if you intend to do something about it. But you can't keep putting it off. Regardless of what age you are, you aren't getting any younger. It's fun to decide to have a week of real listening. You can keep a percentage picture in your mind. Decide in advance that when you're with younger people, you are going to listen and talk no more than a fair percentage of the time.

Some good listeners talk only 10 percent of the time. Maybe you want to set a maximum of 20 percent. But the challenge, however, is to listen much more than you talk.

As a guide, you should remember that if four people are present, you're individually entitled to talk only 25 percent of the time. Many people, once they get past 50, forget this. They make the mistake of thinking that young people are so hungry for their wisdom, that it entitles the older person to talk far more than he or she listens.

Not so.

If you want to become the kind of older person that young people like, you must be willing to listen to them.

What a nice legacy Charles Roth left to us—the awareness that older people can be good listeners and how much it can mean when they are.

Getting Back to Basics

Some years ago, I surveyed a great many young people as to what it was they disliked about older people. Quite often, they demonstrated, often violently, that they didn't dislike older people. They often referred to a relative, often a specific relative, and expressed sentiments about the love they felt for that person. Someone whom they liked immensely. It happened often enough to represent a hopeful sign.

The growing awareness in the 90s as to our increased life expectancy has made young people more aware of the fact that they, too, will be "older people" and for a much longer time than their grandparents were. Young people no longer dislike older people automatically, if they ever did. They do, however, intensely dislike some of the things that too many older people do. Listen to the way one younger person put it.

"Actually, I like older people," she began. She went on to rave about her grandmother who was over 70, but kept up with the new books, television programs, and politics. It's her criticism, however, that we can learn from.

"Most older people seem to resist new ideas," she said. "I don't mean accepting new ideas, I mean discussing them." She could see me mulling over the difference, so she went on.

"Young people don't really mind that they can't convince older people that things are different now, and that philosophies and attitudes might have to change. What a lot of my friends and I object to about older people is that they won't even discuss some things, much less with an open mind."

Why is it that new ideas seem more dangerous to us when we get to be 60 or 70 or 80? They don't seem more dangerous to adopt, but more dangerous to discuss. What's wrong with discussing sex? Why can so few older people discuss rationally the idea of young people living together before marriage, even though it has become prevalent in the last 20 years? I said discuss it, not accept the idea. Why is it that so few older people find it impossible to share their wisdom about sexual matters with the young?

And, how can parents and grandparents, as they look back 20 years ago to the early '70s, justify the closed minds they had about even things like long hair, or the short skirts of today. Many were smoking cigarettes and drinking alcohol, but had closed minds about things like marijuana. Older people can justify not approving it's use at that time; it's harder, however, to justify the closed minds so many of them had and in many cases, still have. So closed, in fact, that they wouldn't, and often still won't, discuss it with their children.

You don't need to change your ideas just to get young people to like you. Many of them appreciate the fact that older people have standards that are consistent. What they resent is your unwillingness to treat them as adults and talk about some of those things they want to talk about.

It can be helpful to review the closed minds that you may have had in the '60s and '70s if only to remind you how important it is that you don't have those same closed minds during the 1990s.

There are other things to guard against, too. Some of your contemporaries let themselves become sloppy and even smelly. They wear dirty clothes and apparently are too lazy to bathe frequently, shave often enough, or go to the beauty parlor. Yet, they still wonder why young people don't treat them with respect.

You have an obligation to be the kind of older person that young people like. You have an obligation to look like the kind of person they will want to listen to.

Why?

Because you have something to say . . . and they need to hear it. You can certainly do something about the thinking directed against you and the remarks that might be made about you. Show that you have an open mind instead of the closed mind so often associated with older people. And you shouldn't wait until you are 60 or 70 to do so.

Here is a tip on how to go about having a more open mind about some of the things being looked at and discussed today. First, be more interested in discussing the things with which you don't agree. Not because you're interested in changing minds, but merely because it is good to be reminded that most things have at least two sides. The other side can be interesting also.

Second, you need to form the habit of reacting more positively and less negatively. Your initial reaction doesn't commit you irrevocably. Whether you react negatively or positively can be followed by thoughtful appraisal. An automatic negative reaction loses points for you, but a positive one gains points for you. Reacting positively takes practice, but that's all, really.

Third, you need to preface your questions or challenges to young people and others with a complimentary remark of some kind. There are so many things they deserve to be complimented for.

These three things can make you feel better and healthier.

The Importance of Not Talking Too Much

Sometime ago, Dear Abby ran a letter in her column in which she quoted a 70 year old grandmother as saying, "Yesterday, my older son took me aside and said, "Mother, I don't want to hurt your feelings, but you talk too much." She wrote that she was so hurt she wanted to die. She had become self-conscious and unhappy because of her new awareness of how often she had been guilty of talking too much.

"How does one find the happy medium?" she asked Abby. As usual, Dear Abby's answer contained two wonderful suggestions. First, only talk when you have something of consequence to say. Second, resolve never to interrupt anyone.

Her excellent advice may be a little hard to follow for some people who seem to spend all their time gossiping or talking about things that are of no consequence. We'd like to remind you of a third suggestion. One that will give the talker, even the compulsive talker, a guide to go by. It can be a useful formula and you'll be remembered for it.

"Talk only your share."

Don't try to complicate it. Keep it simple. We're back to our percentages. If there is only one person with you you are entitled to talk 50 percent of the time. There are exceptions, of course, if someone has asked to come over to tell you his or her news or problems, you have to give up your share, or most of it.

When there are three people present, you are individually entitled to talk only one-third of the time, ordinarily, that is. Most of the time, if there are other people present, you don't need to feel guilty about talking 20 percent of the time.

Being aware of this balance quickly becomes easy and fun. Instead of being the one who is losing friends because of talking too much, you can become the aware one. A side benefit quickly shows up in your conversational habits. You become more careful of what you say and you become one of those people to whom others will listen. You start to do almost automatically what Abby advises. In other words, not talking unless you have something worth saying.

Conversational awareness has other benefits besides helping you be the kind of person everyone likes. One of these is that you become a better listener. As a good listener you can reap some very interesting dividends that are much more important as you get older. You become someone other people want to talk to. Not a person they want to avoid. The good listeners are the ones whose advice is asked most often, and that is satisfying.

Of course, the conscientious talker who wants to talk only a fair share of the time, does occasionally run into the untalkative clam. There is a two-word secret for handling that situation. Those of you already using it know the enjoyment it gives to bring out someone like this and how grateful to you they often become. The secret?

Ask questions.

No matter how hard you look, you'll find few better secrets for being the kind of older person everyone likes, and the kind who leaves a legacy of value . . . by example!

Remember too, that when we talk about listening, we mean "active listening." It can really cut down on your very peace of mind when you wonder later if you were paying enough attention when someone was talking with you.

8

Do's and Don'ts
to Preserve
Your Peace of Mind

*"People put off making financial decisions
because although they know the problems,
they don't know the solutions."*

But now let's get more into five of the do's and don'ts I rate as the most important for preserving your peace of mind.

First, Do Develop and Maintain the Right Attitude about Aging. I have mentioned it so much you probably aren't surprised that developing the right attitude about getting older and staying well is listed first. Of course, I mean have the right attitude about a great many things.

Second, Do Practice Positive Thinking and Believing. During the 70s and 80s the disparagement of positive thinking became fashionable in some circles, but not with those people, strangely enough, who were staying well and aging more slowly than their fellows. This group seemed to attach a great deal of importance to thinking positive thoughts and indulging in the type of "positive thinking" that Dr. Norman Vincent Peale had continued to write so lucidly about. Disparage it if you will, but it might be smarter if instead we are to dust off our copy of *The Power of Positive Thinking* by Dr. Peale and read it again. Or if you can find that other special book, the one by Claude Bristol titled *The Magic of Believing,* by all means read it.

Third, Don't Neglect Exercise, Recreation, and Sex. Surprisingly, authorities say that sex is not just okay for older people, but actually recommended. Of course, doctors have been recommending other forms of recreation for many years. They have proven with impressive medical studies that healthful recreation and exercise is essential to the physical and mental health of the average older person.

You shouldn't delude yourself that sitting around doing nothing or watching television is what doctors recommend as healthful recreation. Most people do enough of that without doctors advocating it. Still, television can be a great reward after you've done some of the other activities that can play a larger role in recreating a healthy mind and healthy body. These healthy activities may include hiking, running, biking, reading, golf, tennis, sightseeing, and so on. You'll notice I didn't list anything that allows sitting down (except biking and reading). But only because most people do enough sitting down activities (only very few of which are healthful,) without any help from authors.

Fourth, Do Cut Down on Your Eating and Drinking. There is so much said and written about this that we're going to leave number four at that. Just do it.

Fifth, Don't Let Yourself Stay Depressed for Too Long a Period of Time. Of course, as you get older you are going to feel depressed occasionally. We all do and it is psychologically very important that you keep this in mind. Everyone feels depressed occasionally, even if it's only relative.

Feelings of depression are bad only when they persist or occur too often. What you need to do first is recognize your depressions and have a way to get out of them.

Being depressed is bad enough. Feeling guilty and worrying about it is what does most of the damage. So don't worry. Just do something about it. That's what these do's and don'ts are all about.

There are seven things to do, by the way, that help.

First, try to put the blame on yourself a little less often.

Second, talk things over rather than let things bother you and go on gnawing at you.

Third, don't let other people put a burden on you because of what they expect of you, especially if it is more than they have the right to expect.

Fourth, change whatever is making you feel depressed if it is in your power. But accept it if you can do nothing about it.

Fifth, distinguish between your needs and wants. If your needs are not being met, it is understandable to be upset and maybe even depressed. But your wants deserve a lower priority. There are other strategies that help. When you find successful strategies, you should make a list and use them the next time you are feeling depressed.

Sixth, accept yourself. That doesn't mean you shouldn't try to improve. One of the most thought-provoking bits of advice that came out of the growth and human potential movement of the '60s was usually put this way: "Accept yourself the way you are." Some of us raised with the Christian work ethic and the self-improvement philosophy didn't give much credit to the lazy person who expected a lot of brownie points merely for accepting the fact that he or she was lazy. I am inclined to think that it might be necessary to recognize it, maybe even admit to being lazy, but accepting instead of doing something about it rubbed me the wrong way.

An old friend, George Dovenmeuhle, at one time a top therapist in Denver, taught me a valuable lesson. He said, "I want to show my years gracefully, but I'm proud of having lived them." What was special about George, and still is, is that he didn't stop with accepting the fact that he was growing older. He ate very lightly, drank only moderately, and exercised daily. People who do nothing but accept themselves the way they are deserve some credit, but those who accept themselves the way they are and try to improve, deserve even more credit.

Seventh, have standards to live by. Those of you who lived through the 1940s and 1950s probably remember a great number of self-help books, articles, and records that exhorted us to "aim for the stars," told us in no uncertain terms that "Man's reach should exceed his grasp." Many of them went on to remind us in stimulating prose that "there is no magic in small goals" and made us feel foolish if we tended to settle for only improvement when they were convinced that "anything that Man can visualize, he can accomplish."

We were even made to feel inadequate. "Dream the Impossible Dream." Most of these authors had some wonderfully good ideas, but also a perfectionist philosophy that kept many people from even improving.

This striving for perfection can be deadly. Our mental hospitals are filled with perfectionists who are never able to live up to their unrealistic performance standards. Our nursing homes and convalescent hospitals are filled with people living out their lives in quiet regret. Personal growth doesn't stop just because we have reached that age of 60, 70, or 80.

There is something that older people can aim for and motivate themselves with that is far better and more effective than aiming for perfection. This is aiming for *improvement.* If and when that loses the power to motivate you, there is something else you can aim for better than perfection. That is superiority. Excellence. Excellence is something you can achieve. It is usually a relative thing. Excellence can often be compared to what someone else does. It has human parameters unlike perfection which challenges the mind to disprove. Excellence lends itself to an objective appraisal whether it concerns something you have done or that someone else has done. It is much easier to assess fairly when you are trying to categorize something as good or excellent. The perfectionist lives constantly with a sense of failure. How can one help it? For the discriminating person, it is in most areas of our lives, impossible to attain. Failing to attain it not only offers no satisfaction, it is counter-productive. Instead of adding to your confidence, as does the feeling you get from improving, the falling short of perfection destroys it and undermines your sense of self-worth.

You shouldn't be a perfectionist . . . particularly you shouldn't let that type of perfectionist thinking color your memories. Don't be frustrated that your life doesn't measure up to some ridiculous standard you set for yourself. Reminisce positively, not negatively. Concentrate on the things you *did* accomplish, not on the failures or things you left undone—a good habit to preserve health.

You shouldn't give yourself a daily assault of the negative. Be willing to subject yourself to other people's negative output (You know, the constant complaining about their health or the sad state of their world or how ungrateful everybody is or how bad the food is or how high prices are). If necessary, you have to be willing to disagree. While you have an obligation to try to change the subject, if that doesn't work, the obligation you have to yourself should require you to terminate that negative input one way or another even if it means an argument.

The habit of dwelling on the positive and striving for *excellence* instead of *perfection* might well be one of the most valuable legacies you could leave.

I have been talking about the do's and don'ts and maybe there are too many things to guard against. Too few things are available to increase the positive effect our mental activities can have on keeping us well. Here are two, however, that you may want to consider.

Get in and do things.

Volunteer.

Say yes when asked. Look for things in which to become involved. Don't be afraid to put forth extra effort. Join. Enroll. Visit. These are things to do for your mental health, for your own happiness.

Now, one last reminder, the truth. We all know the satisfaction that comes from helping other people. It is no secret that it is one of the most effective happiness factors. You need to invest your experience wisely and generously in younger people. You shouldn't be selfish about your discretionary income. As older people, you have contacts and should be willing to solve problems and create opportunities for others. You need to listen more. You can be more involved, not less. Those of you who are involved with other people in a helpful way are smart. You are laying the ground work for leaving valuable legacies.

These are the kinds of positive legacies by which to be remembered. Establishing such legacies can keep you healthier and give you peace of mind.

9

Legacies
for Living

*"Most people live in the cobwebs of whether
or not to have a living trust."*

Some of the things I want to talk about now will be on the subject of money. Some of my comments, however, will be aimed at helping you leave to those you care about what I've chosen to call "Legacies of Wisdom."

There is a spending by choice technique, which many of you don't really need, but most of our younger friends, relatives, employees, and others do need very badly.

The 1980s, was a period in which the baby-boomers over-spent and lavishly abused their credit cards. They became good at spending money but not at spending money wisely.

There are few how-to-live legacies that you can leave to those you care about which are more valuable than good buying habits or wisdom about spending money. And as those of you who are over 50 know, how you spend your money plays a greater role in how much wealth you accumulate than how you invest your money.

More Legacies

There has been a lot of criticism in the 1990s about this country's educational system and what it isn't teaching. Perhaps most bothersome to those of us in the financial services industry are two things that should be deeply embedded in the awareness of all students finishing their academic education. One: for the saving they should do, is the time-value of money, in other words the power of compound interest. And two: for the investing they should graduate to, is the power of dollar-cost averaging.

You may want to help other younger people become aware of the power of compound interest and dollar-cost-averaging for saving and investing.

First, however, I'll discuss very briefly the other of the big five of personal finance besides saving and investing. These, by the way are spending, insuring, and planning.

I have already talked some about spending. Now I'll talk about saving, using compound interest, and doing conceptual estate planning.

The most basic goal of saving is to have enough money in the bank to take care of the sudden emergencies that so often arise.

The most basic rule about insurance is to have enough. It is second only to a readily available nest egg in a savings account. With the progressive life insurance programs of today this is easy, although the argument is still going on about "term and cash value" life insurance.

The old-line executives deserved criticism in the 1960s. In the 1980s, however, newer and more progressive executives in the insurance industry improved their policies and reduced the cost of what they were offering the consumer. Next to the computer industry, and perhaps the shoe industry, the insurance industry has done the most to improve what it is now offering the consumer. Insurance and annuity policies are now capable of solving financial problems far beyond merely guarding against emergencies.

Investment Strategies: Not Always the Same

Your investing strategy should change as you get older. You should approach investments differently if you're 70 or 80 than you would if you were 20 or 30. Some basic rules still apply, however. One is that you need to know your "risk-tolerance." In other words, the maximum amount of risk with which you're comfortable. Two, is that you need to know the power of dollar-cost averaging. Three, is that greater investment returns almost always involve greater risk and are a health factor.

Financial planning has always been done by very wealthy people and it is often credited with being responsible for the wealth they accumulated. Sophisticated financial planning for "Mr. and Mrs. Average American" only became popular in the '70s with the creation of the certified financial planner program. It was accelerated in the '80s with the chartered financial consultant training made available by the American College in Bryn Mawr. Financial planning was used widely in the '80s as a way to avoid taxes while building an estate. There is evidence that in the '90s it is also getting back to where the emphasis was in the '70s, in other words, as a way to accumulate money for those who don't have it.

Conceptual estate planning is more. It is aimed at not only building an estate, but also designed to accomplish what the client wants and needs in life as well as death.

Why use a financial professional? It is true, of course, that many sophisticated investors know as much about investing as any financial planner they might work with. There are some clients who know as much about insurance as the insurance agent they work with. Conceptual estate planning, however, takes in all of the big five of personal finance. It also leads to building an estate for retirement as well as for passing on. There are very few people other than financial professionals who have made a study of all of those five.

One other advantage of dealing with a financial professional over the do-it-yourself approach—what you as clients do not have which you can often find with a financial professional is "objectivity." People have heard me say, "Beware of those who say they can be objective about their money. They will lie about other things, also."

Having a financial advisor to help you plan ahead can play an important part in preserving not only your wealth but also your *peace of mind.*

There are really painful regrets that haunt people who have labored for years to acquire money and other assets and have built up a valuable estate only to see it shrink because of poor management.

The other people I feel sorry for are those who hear themselves saying "I didn't know that!" or "why didn't someone tell me!" or "how could I have been so stupid!"

Of course, there are those, after you have passed on, who might say "how could he (or she) have been so thoughtless?" Or they might say "why didn't she (or he) do a little estate planning?"

There are these people, thousands of them. They are the reason I was so glad that Kim Ciccarelli Banta, an outstandingly capable financial and estate planner, would co-author this book and share with you the most vital aspects of this estate planning book.

You'll find in her advice, for which many of her clients willingly pay thousands of dollars, not only valuable information for preserving your family wealth, but helpful ideas for accumulating it.

PART II

For You and Your Children

This section of Preserving Family Wealth & Peace of Mind *is designed to introduce you to some of the problems that exist when you wish to pass on your assets to your heirs. You will read about ways of reducing erosion of the estate, proper methods for preservation, and supportive ways to achieving estate objectives.*

Estate Planning is long term—its impact reaches out beyond the span of an individual life and covers future generations and your favorite charities. Professional Estate Planning requires an understanding of the tax tables so they may benefit you. Estate Planning is a personal matter. It is the review of the estate you created, the children you have raised, their needs and financial capabilities, your spouse's interest and ability in preserving your standard of living, and your capital. It is a "charted" or distribution pattern that covers the recipient of your estate and the manner in which you wish it to be distributed.

There are many legacies we wish to leave our children. Our estate is one of the most important.

10

This Is the Time of Your Life

" I would like to prepare my children for the responsibility of having assets. "

There is no better way to describe good estate planning, but that of the deep feeling of relief you experience when your affairs have been successfully put in order for your sake, and the sake of loved ones who survive you. Estate planning is a continuous and perpetual motion that moves assets, philosophies, and attitudes through generations of descendants.

Most people I work with aim not only to provide for the adequate and efficient transfer of assets to chosen heirs, but also to shield their family from the unnecessary burden of taking care of them in years to come. You are probably one of many people that do not want to be a liability to your children in later years.

People who fail to make provisions do not suffer. Their heirs and loved ones suffer. If you die without proper estate planning documents, you may, without intent, partially disinherit your spouse or perhaps condemn your estate to an unnecessarily prolonged and expensive process called probate. Estate taxes can erode as much as 55 to 60 percent of your assets. Without a good estate plan, your intentions may *never* be carried out. A strong objective certainly may be to insure that the wealth you intended to pass to your heirs does so, under the distribution plan you set up. Will the documents you executed do exactly as you had desired in your heart? Have you titled your assets appropriately so that they will to be distributed under the provisions in your documents?

If tax laws or family circumstances change, then continue to update your written intentions to mirror your objectives. Nine to ten percent of the estate planning process is "startup"; more importantly, 90 percent is continuous, perpetual updating and servicing. Here, your advisor's role is the key. Your legal, tax, and financial professionals should constructively work with you to ensure the proper plan. For your family's benefit, continuously make your advisors aware of any personal or financial changes that could alter the handling of your affairs.

Today your problem may be in how to pass your estate; tomorrow it could be in how to keep your assets whole through sickness or at the loss of your spouse.

This is the time of *your* life. This is "retirement," the quest for peace, time, and the economic substance to enjoy all those things you like to do. As people mature, they develop an awareness for those realities in life which they cannot control:

> "I never looked forward to or understood that the other people around me, my friends and family, would be aging" (A grieving sister).

> "I truly believed money was relatively unimportant. Now I know that the only way to keep money unimportant is to have it and plan properly, so that my time can be spent with the real priorities of life—my children, my family, our health." (A recently widowed man).

Money doesn't alleviate the tragedies of life, but it does enable you to handle them better. The priority of money decisions later is based on how you manage your affairs today.

Each day, time becomes more valuable, as the probability of death is more imminent. With limitations on the energies you can expend, you must carefully think out each decision necessary to continue your required lifestyles, and ultimately pass on your values and financial assets to your families.

Are you a person who does not make a decisive estate plan for one of three reasons:

1. You are unaware of the problems evolving due to the nature and size of your assets.
2. You know you have a problem, but are confused about the solution. You don't know who to turn to or where to start.

3. You have been mislead before. Because of your initial experience you continue to put off financial decisions and never assume responsibility for the assets you have accumulated.

You must spend the proper time and attention your assets and peace of mind deserve. *Each estate, no matter what size it is, warrants a plan.* It would be impossible for individuals on their own, to develop the proficient knowledge that is necessary for current estate solutions. Change occurs rapidly and sporadically. Solutions are whimsical due to government legislation and acceptability. Timely, well programmed strategies require the type of knowledge that only a network of competent professional advisors can provide.

Should you use a financial advisor to assist in the estate planning process? Perhaps a sensible explanation for why you should coordinate your planning with a financial professional is the objectivity and summary of experiences, legalities, and responsibilities they can share with you to support your own decision making. This additional interpretation of information can create a well-thought out plan. When working with several clients, consultants are exposed through evaluation and decision making to the many successes and failures their clients have experienced and why they may have happened. People are more inclined to dismiss personal financial failures and seldom share the route and agony to how success occurs. The sharing of prior experiences can be valuable in developing a comfortable and proper path for your family. Wouldn't you like to understand why some people go through very little financial and emotional trauma in the distribution or inheritance of an estate?

Your time and your homework should be seriously spent in choosing and selecting your professional advisors rather than trying to know all the answers. Your professional team will instruct you through the necessary education, motivation, and execution relative to your affairs.

Work with a team of advisors. It is impossible to put a value on the benefit and importance of working with competent financial professionals as a team. For instance, your financial counselor can be instrumental in coordinating the expertise and services of your legal and tax advisors. Leveraging their time may provide a more cost efficient, effective planning solution.

Read what you can on the topic of Estate Planning, Living Trusts, Supertrusts, Family Gifting, and Living Wills. The apparent defect is that these sources cannot be as current or individualized as what your advisor will share with you first hand; but there is reliable, good information that can preliminarily guide you. Estate planning, a very personalized process, must be tailored to you from the beginning through to the final stages of the plan.

I truly believe most people are capable of making good decisions given the proper facts. Our role as financial professionals is to present the facts. Your role is to take responsibility for your assets and execute good decisions. Don't procrastinate because the problems you encounter today may only grow more intense tomorrow.

When you find someone capable who you are comfortable with, and who you feel has your best interest at heart, then you can expect the relationship to be beneficial to both parties. How a professional profits is relatively unimportant. It may be through legal fees, financial advisory fees, or being named broker of record and receiving commissions. *What matters is value.* The value received is umbrellaed in the plan you establish, which should invariably result in the solution most suitable for your estate. The choice of the professional(s) who will be involved in your planning, is most essential and should be your first criteria.

To do nothing regarding your financial matters is the worst decision you could make. The following chapters are designed to take a complex and often terribly neglected subject, estate planning, and stimulate you to act, take care of your affairs, and protect yourself and your family against the risk of living too long, or dying too soon. Do what needs to be done—*now.*

From My Clients' Files:

"We wished we had acted sooner. It was just last Thursday we promised the attorney we would come in and sign. It's now too late, my husband died at 4:00 this morning."

The attorney and the client's heirs have more time and work ahead of them because the couple didn't execute what they had talked about for years. We were not able to utilize a very important tax savings. It's unfortunate, but remember there is still time for the wife to be sure the ultimate heirs don't incur the same financial and time restraints that can be so emotionally devastating at the time of her passing.

Who Is Your
Unwritten Beneficiary?

---

*"Most people fail to take advantage of
the estate tax tables."*

You are permitted to accumulate assets, but don't accumulate too many. That is, unless you are expecting to set up a tax efficient distribution plan.

Step one is being knowledgeable about the taxes and probate costs that will be a liability to your estate and which are generally due within nine months from the date of your death. Perhaps the reason why less than 30 percent of the population set up proper estate planning documents is because they are unaware of these existing circumstances. You may be familiar with the many forms of taxation but you must also understand that two of the most destructive taxes in our system are federal estate taxes and state inheritance taxes.

The federal estate tax is a progressive tax starting at 37 percent and increasing to 60 percent. On top of this, we may have to pay out state estate or inheritance taxes, GST Taxes (Generation Skipping Taxes), and Excise taxes on pension benefits. The federal tax is assessed against every asset that is passed on to your survivors at death. There are two exceptions that are available to every United States citizen:

1. The Unlimited Marital Deduction

There is an "unlimited marital deduction" allowing assets to pass between spouses with no Federal tax liability incurred. Probate costs may exist with any transfer of assets, including between spouses, and this area is covered in detail in THE PITFALLS OF ESTATE PLANNING WITH "JOINT TENANCY ONLY" by Joseph Ferraina in Part III.

Look at an example of what happens when a spouse decides to pass on her assets to her husband through an "I Love You" Simple Will plan, or by titling every account in joint names.We are demonstrating what happens when the husband dies first:

Husband's Estate of $800,000 passes to the Wife under an "I Love You Will." The IRS liability is $0 because of the unlimited marital deduction, but, the Wife's Estate is worth $400,000 with her assets alone. Combining $800,000 from the Husband's Estate, and $400,000 of her own assets, $1,200,000 in total assets are now titled in her name after the death of her husband. The result is, that the surviving wife's taxable estate is $1,200,000.

The biggest problem with this type of planning is that you are losing a second very valuable exception to our Federal estate tax system under the laws implemented in the early '80s. Under this scenario, taxes would be due at the surviving spouse's death of $235,000+.

Planning could have been done to prevent this by taking advantage of the husband's unified credit.

2. The Unified Credit

In addition to the marital deduction, each person is entitled to a unified credit that allows one to pass up to $600,000 in assets during his or her lifetime or at death to whomever he or she chooses. In the above example, the husband set up an ineffective distribution plan because he used only his unlimited marital deduction to pass his assets. His estate lost the use of the unified credit by not preserving it at his death. This type of estate plan caused the wife's estate to be taxable to the children at her death. This estate shrinkage is the amount that goes to your unwritten beneficiary, the Internal Revenue Service. If the family in this example had executed their documents properly and completed the necessary asset repositioning, this loss to the IRS could have been avoided. The entire $1,200,000 would pass to their heirs estate tax free under current tax laws!

We're going to talk more about the tax efficient plan in our chapter on living trusts.

A person's intelligence, financial, career success, and/or family and personal life successes, have little to do with the effectiveness of their chosen estate strategies. It takes perseverance and a willingness to openly discuss the question *"What do I want to happen when I am no longer here?"*

Several of the most sophisticated people of our times have failed to properly plan for the distribution of their estate. The examples in Chart 1 are of some prominent people who perhaps neglected to think that the legacies they were to pass on deserved the proper time and attention it takes to prepare an estate for ultimate distribution to their heirs! We have learned of their errors by obtaining the "Public Record" of their estate settlements. Probate is a matter of public record (see Chart 1 at the end of this chapter).

Please don't make mistakes that can be avoided when passing your legacy on. What you have worked hard to accumulate should be preserved according to your wishes and the distribution of this wealth well instructed in your completed documents.

Remember step one is an understanding of the tax tables and how they work. Then, add up your net worth. Include every item that can be valued monetarily:

Bank accounts
Securities accounts
Mutual Funds
Annuities
Bearer Bonds in your safe deposit box
Qualified Plans (monthly survivorship benefits, present value
   & lump sums)
Cash
Money markets
Real estate and royalty interests
Business interests
Residences
Tangible personal property
Inheritances or trusts
Life insurance (death benefit if you are the insured, cash value if you
   are listed as the owner)

Next, determine your tax liability according to the Federal Tax Laws. Chart 2 at the end of this chapter illustrates the tables in effect as of the early 1990s.

Resident Alien

If your surviving spouse is a non-U.S. citizen, then special planning must be done. Resident aliens are entitled to only a $100,000/year transfer of assets from their spouse or $100,000 at death, free from federal estate taxation. Here, it is not only the distribution to the children that may be taxed, but the transfer of assets between spouses. Prior to the passing of a revenue act in 1988, a non-U.S. citizen resident spouse qualified for the estate tax marital deduction. The government caught wind of the fact that estate taxes were not only being deferred, but under the above scenario, were sometimes lost forever. If the non-citizen, surviving spouse left the U.S. and was beyond the taxing jurisdiction at the time of his or her death, then only property actually in the U.S. at this time could be taxed. The loophole was closed. This area has become quite complicated. Property that rightfully belongs to the surviving non-citizen spouse must be proven as such, and full consideration must have been given from their own funds.

Planning to pass assets through a special trust, namely a Qualified Domestic Trust (QDT) can permit deferral of taxes on the first spouse to die. The document must be meticulously drafted and the assets titled properly. Work closely with your attorney here, as this is a case where the surviving spouse cannot be named directly as the trustee or a co-trustee. The trustee of a QDT trust must be an individual citizen of the United States or domestic corporation. The trust *must distribute* all income to the surviving spouse. In addition, a taxable event can occur if there is any distribution of property to the spouse other than income. In many cases, non-citizen resident spouses are becoming United States citizens to alleviate this unnecessary tax burden.

State Death Taxes

Where you live also determines what additional taxes your estate will incur. Mr. Stephen P. Bauer, in his article, WHEN WE TALK ABOUT PASSING ON OUR ESTATE TO OUR CHILDREN, WHAT IS THE ROLE OF THE STATE IN WHICH WE RESIDE? addresses the important and timely issue of residency. Be sure to read it thoroughly if you have changed your state of residence. The state where you now reside, or the state in which you previously resided, may be entitled to a share of the assets or legacy you wish to pass on. This is often the case when a client has tried to change his or her residency. Most states in our country have incorrectly budgeted their revenue and they are making up for it by collecting taxes upon death. Many people are unaware of this tax and consequently don't vote against levying up this tax. There are numerous estates that have been taxed by two, three, and four different states that have made claims against the assets. The Howard Hughes Estate is a perfect example. There have been incidences in case law where very little or nothing was left for the heirs. Ask whether there is a tax in the state of domicile, and if so, is it a "pickup" tax? A "pickup" tax means, in essence, that your estate incurs a maximum liability to the tune of the Federal taxes due, but a portion is paid out to the state of residency instead. This is the method the State of Florida uses for its estate tax. With any of the other states, you need to determine if an additional tax is due over and above the gross federal estate tax liability.

Some of these states where this may be the case include: Connecticut, Mississippi, Delaware, Nebraska, Indiana, New York, Iowa, North Carolina, Kansas, Ohio, Kentucky, Oklahoma, Louisiana, Pennsylvania Maryland, Rhode Island, Massachusetts, South Carolina, Michigan, South Dakota, Wisconsin.

Probate

Have you known anyone who has gone through the tedious, timely, costly, and emotional disruption of probate? I am silently angered when a grieving widow's adjustment to the death of her husband includes the agony of settling his estate through probate and public administration. More often than not this could have been simply and justifiably avoided.

There is no explanation or excuse for the noncompletion of a basic estate plan to pass assets easily and privately between spouses. Today there is a multitude of information available on the topic of estate planning. Perhaps it is a reluctance to talk about death, but the realization exists that your plan covers lifetime risks which may be ever increasingly important. Perhaps, it is an untimely death. Most deaths are untimely. Be prepared, at the very least, by doing the proper planning that you, and only you, have control over. Is your age 50, 60, 70, 80, or 90? Was there no time that could have been devoted to eliminate the strenuous financial and emotional burdens for your heirs that happens when settling an estate that had not been cared for properly?

You cannot help to ease the pain or suffering at the death of a loved one, but you do have the ability to make it easier by taking care of tedious, cumbersome details beforehand. Only then is your legacy truly a gift of love. Assets may be more comfortably passed on to your spouse, and on again, perhaps through generations of family and friends and even charity. Familiarize yourself with some of the executor's duties and discuss them with your advisors. Is there any step you may avoid or simplify by preparing for the ultimate transfer of your legacy today?

Preliminary List of Executor Duties

1. Probate of Will.
2. Advertise Grant of Letters.
3. Inventory of safe deposit box.
4. Claim for life insurance benefits, obtain Form 712 from insurance company.
   a. Consider mode of payment.
5. Claim for pension and profit sharing benefits.
   a. Consider mode of payment.
   b. Obtain copies of plan, IRS approval, and beneficiary designation.
6. Apply for lump sum Social Security benefits and VA benefits.
7. File Form 56 Notice of Fiduciary Relationship.
8. Open estate checking and savings accounts.
9. Write to banks for date of death value.
10. Value securities.
11. Appraisal of real property and personal property.
12. Obtain 3 years of U.S. individual income tax returns and 3 years of canceled checks.
13. Obtain 5 year financials on business interest plus all relevant agreements.
14. Obtain copies of all U.S. gift tax returns filed by decedent.
15. Obtain evidence of all debts of decedent and costs of administering estate.
16. Were any of decedent's medical expenses unpaid at death?
17. Has the estate received after death income taxable under Section 691 of the IRC?
18. Prepayment of state inheritance tax. Check state law to determine if permissible, are there advantages and if so, the applicable deadlines.

19. File personal property tax returns due February 15 of each year estate is in administration.
20. Consider requesting prompt assessment of decedent's U.S. income taxes.
21. File final U.S. (IRS Form 1040) and state individual tax return due April 15th for the year in which death occurs; and gift tax returns due by the time estate tax return is due.
22. Is the estate subject to ancillary administration?
23. Are administration expenses and losses to be claimed as an income or estate tax deduction?
24. Obtain alternate valuation date values for federal estate tax return.
25. Payment of U.S. estate tax with flower bonds must be tendered to Federal Reserve within 9 months of death.
26. Consider election of extension of time to pay U.S. estate tax (Sections 6161 or 6166) which must be filed on or before due date of U.S. estate tax returns including extensions.
27. Consider election to defer payment of inheritance tax on remainder interests where permitted, detemine deadline for election.
28. File form notice to IRS required by Section 6039A of IRS due with final U.S. individual income tax return or U.S. estate tax return.
29. Elect (or do not elect) to qualify certain terminable interest property for marital deduction.
30. Ascertain if credit for tax or prior transfers are allowable.
31. File inheritance and federal estate tax return due within 9 months of death. Extensions may be requested. Check local state law for due date and possible extension.
32. File inventory. Check local state law for requirements and due date.
33. Apply for U.S. I.D. number if estate will file U.S. income tax returns.
34. Consider redemption under IRS Section 303.
35. Apply for tax waivers.
36. File account or prepare informal family agreement.
37. Prepare audit notices and statement of proposed distribution.
38. File schedule of distribution if applicable.

I can only suggest to you that the estate tax in many ways is a voluntary tax. If you are a parent or spouse who is concerned, then take an aggressive stance to reduce taxes, probate and administrative expenses. Remember it was Judge Learned Hand who said:

> Anyone may so arrange his affairs that his taxes shall be as low as possible; he is not bound to choose that pattern which will best pay the Treasury; there is not even a patriotic duty to increase one's taxes. [*Helvering v. Gregory*, 69 F.2d 809, 810 (1934)].

From My Clients' Files:

"He was always the one who took care of everything. Now they tell me I have to value everything we own. We never listed accounts and numbers. I'm not sure where all our dividend checks come from. This will take me months and months. My attorney says I must have it done soon so they may complete filing with the IRS within the nine month period. This is July. I'm supposed to get this information by September 9th. My children need me now. No one has explained all this to me. Can you help me?"

Take time now to sit down with the person you have named executor of your estate and your heirs. Prepare for the consequences when your assets must pass on. You do not have to detail what you have or what you are worth; just summarize generalities of your plan, and let your family know where to go for the information when you die. In working with our clients, we prepare a confidential detailed listing of assets and account numbers not less than annually. It is in our clients' hands then to determine when they wish to share this information with their children. If this will not be done, the children are introduced to us and our firm and know to call us first when a death or disability occurs.

CHART 1

The Attorney - Albert Picard
Prominent Attorney - San Francisco, California - Died Intestate

Gross Estate	$1,003,599
Total Costs	$486,737
Net Estate	$516,862

Over 48% Shrinkage of Estate Remaining to Pass to be Divided Amongst the Heirs

Settlement Costs:

Debts	$159,301
Administration Expense	6,197
Attorney's Fee	19,999
Administrator's Fee	19,999
Accountant's Fee	7,000
California Inheritance Tax	64,025
Federal Estate Tax	210,216
TOTAL COSTS	**$486,737**

The Accountant - Alwin Charles Ernst
Senior Partner - Ernst & Ernst, Accountants - Cleveland, Ohio
Died at age 66, Intestate (No Will)

Gross Estate	$12,642,431
Total Costs	$7,124,112
Net Estate	$5,518,319

Over 56% Shrinkage

Settlement Costs:

Debts	$6,232
Administration Expense	58,862
Attorney's Fee	10,000
Executor's Fee	10,000
Ohio Inheritance Tax	1,226,737
Federal Estate Tax	5,812,281
TOTAL COSTS	**$7,124,112**

The Celebrity - Elvis Presley
Memphis, Tennessee - Died at age 42

Gross Estate	$10,165,635
Total Costs	$7,374,635
Net Estate	$2,790,790

Over 73% Shrinkage

Settlement Costs:

Debts	$3,832,552
Administration Expense	114,563
Attorney's Fee	18,000
Executor's Fee	70,000
Tennessee Inheritance Tax	526,435
California Inheritance Tax	27,500
Federal Estate Tax	2,374,635
TOTAL COSTS	**$7,374,635**

The President - Franklin Delano Roosevelt
Residence, Hyde Park, New York - Died at age 63

Gross Estate	$1,940,999
Total Costs	$574,867
Net Estate	$1,366,132

Over 29% Shrinkage

Settlement Costs:

Debts	$19,221
Administration Expense	35,022
Attorney's Fee	75,000
Executor's Fee	99,494
New York Estate Tax	48,480
Federal Estate Tax	297,650
TOTAL COSTS	**$574,867**

CHART 2

If the amount with respect to which the tentative tax to be computed is:	The tentative tax is:
Not Over $10,000	18% of such amount.
$10,001-$20,000	$1,800, plus 20% of the excess of such amount over $10,000.
$20,001-$40,000	$3,800, plus 22% of the excess of such amount over $20,000.
$40,001-$60,000	$8200, plus 24% of the excess of such amount over $40,000.
$60,001-$80,000	$13,000, plus 26% of the excess of such amount over $60,000.
$80,001-$100,000	$18,200, plus 26% of the excess of such amount over $80,000.
$100,001-$150,000	$23,800, plus 30% of the excess of such amount over $100,000.
$150,001-$250,000	$38,800, plus 32% of the excess of such amount over $150,000.
$250,001-$500,000	$70,800, plus 34% of the excess of such amount over $250,000.
$500,000-$750,000	$155,800, plus 37% of the excess of such amount over $500,000.
$750,001-$1,000,000	$248,300, plus 39% of the excess of such amount over $750,000.
$1,000,001-$1,250,000	$345,800, plus 41% of the excess of such amount over $1,000,000.
$1,250,001-$1,500,000	$448,300, plus 43% of the excess of such amount over $1,250,000.
$1,500,001-$2,000,000	$555,800, plus 45% of the excess of such amount over $1,500,000.
$2,000,001-$2,250,000	$780,000, plus 49% of the excess of such amount over $2,500,000.
Over $2,500,000	$1,025,800, plus 50% of the excess of such amount over $2,500,000.
$2,500,001-$3,000,000	$1,025,800, plus 53% of the excess of such amount over $2,500,000.
$3,000,001-$3,500,000	$1,290,800, plus 57% of the excess of such amount over $3,500,000.
$3,500,001-$4,000,000	$1,575,800, plus 61% of the excess of such amount over $3,500,000.
Over $4,000,000	$1,880,800, plus 65% of the excess of such amount over $4,000,000.

This table reflects the federal taxes due to the IRS with no plan (only one spouse uses their unified credit) and with a basic tax efficient plan (both spouses take advantage of their $600,000 credit).There is an additional 5% tax imposed on taxable estates over $10,000,000 but less than $21,040,000 to phase out the graduated rate and the unified credit.Therefore, in calculating the applicable rate, the tax may be 60%, not 55%.

12

The Seven Cardinal Mistakes

"We must take responsibility for our assets."

Besides the fact that most people don't have an understanding of the tax tables, there are several other reasons why most people do not gain from their estate planning endeavors. These common obstacles can be expressed as the *Seven Cardinal Mistakes* that prevent most families from preserving and passing on their legacy:

1) Failure to ask the proper questions.

In earlier chapters we discussed the benefit of education through seminars and the value of learning the questions to ask your advisors. Stop searching for the answers first. Your situation is unique and the solution is supposed to fit like a glove. Start at the beginning. Granted, most individuals do not know the questions to ask, don't understand the legal or tax advisor's terminology, and are searching for a way to communicate. A financial professional's best attribute may be working with you to open up the communication process. The professional needs to understand the depth and range of your goals. You need to know the specific questions which need to be asked and answered. With this in mind, your direction will be defined and clarified. Your team of financial, legal, and tax professionals who have years of experience and education behind them, will give you the answers. And remember, every question is worth asking and answering.

2) Failure to plan not only for now but for future circumstances.

Your estate plan must carry on through any time element and must be the solution whenever it is put into effect. If today you have minor or handicapped children, use proper provisions in your documents to designate a caretaker. If you do not, then perhaps it may be left up to the state to determine how and where they will end up. Who will provide for your children, and is this sincerely a decision you wish to put in the hands of our impersonal court system? If today, your estate is not subject to Federal tax liabilities, have you considered how the IRS will value your business or appreciated real estate if you live a long, healthy life, and don't pass your estate until perhaps age 96? Will your heirs be forced to liquidate your estate under an expedient sale in order to pay the taxes due nine months from your date of death? Be realistic when valuing your assets. Include anything that would be included by the IRS. Ask your attorney and advisor to review, in understandable detail, what the IRS reviews when the executor lists your assets. This process will serve to make you better equipped today to handle the shock of taxes due later.

3) Failure to prepare one's spouse.

Perhaps one of the most moving incidences I remember is a male client of mine (age 76, six children) who had taken extensive time to complete his legal documents and then sat down and wrote a long letter to his wife. In the letter, he talked about their life together and how they had committed a lifetime to raising their children, sharing, and building their estate. He apologized for the time they had not jointly spent in setting up their estate plan and the fact that when he was gone, it would be up to her to complete their intentions of passing on their legacy to the children. It would be up to her, as she quietly felt his absence, to learn what needed to be done.

He continued in his letter to explain each step so that she would feel more comfortable with the decisions that would need to be made. These decisions included contacting their financial advisor, attorney, and accountant, listing their total assets and having them formally appraised or valued, and documenting all expenses for final medical care and funeral arrangements. Decisions would need to be made to separate the assets that would be titled into the family trust to preserve his $600,000 credit. This trust would pass to the children estate tax-free when ultimately distributed at her death. Also an assignment of those assets that would pass to her marital trust would need to be completed. This letter only explained some of the technicalities the spouse would face, but it made her feel more at ease and less burdened. I cannot stress enough how important it is for women especially, to commit to sharing with their spouse the planning

71

of legacies as they have committed to sharing a lifetime of experiences.

I give credit to those men who, at elderly ages, take the time to involve their spouses in the financial decisions that need to be made. This is a long, tedious, and often difficult process. Many times, I have been called upon as the medium to turning over a husband's affairs to a wife, or wife in conjunction with a trusted advisor. I applaud those women who commit the energy to learn about and control financial matters they may have never participated in up to this point. The steps you take today can only serve to avoid unintended mishaps later. Remember that estate planning includes not only planning for living a long life but also for the potential complications of incompetency or disability.

4) Failure to update one's documents in accordance with personal or tax law changes.

Executing an estate plan is only part of what will be needed to assure the passing of your legacies according to your intentions. Wills and trusts need to be reviewed at least every other year to be sure that technical provisions or personal provisions have not changed. All estate documents prior to the 1981 law change must be reviewed. Often I hear comments that our "wills/trusts are all in order" only to have them reviewed by an attorney who points out that their residency has changed and their documents do not reflect this, or that their estate is subject to unnecessary taxation because the technical language under the plan is now obsolete. See your attorney or seek out a good estate planning advisor who can assist you in reviewing your current plans.

5) Failure to provide accurate information to the professionals you are working with.

Most professionals cannot and would not provide financial advice or comment on what they feel a client should or shouldn't do unless they know exactly where the client stands. There is an unveiling process that is necessary. Understanding sincerely your objectives, your concerns, your relationships with your children, and your confidence in your children's capability to accept and manage the inherited assets, are all important issues. We must learn to accept and encompass these personal derivatives with your own financial abilities, your medical circumstances, your discretionary cash flow, and expected inheritances. This is essential information which will guide us through the necessary estate planning direction. Chances are, when you complete your estate plan, it may be the first time you look at your entire financial picture. How you pull it all together has great bearing on the effectiveness of your chosen estate solutions.

6) Failure to assess one's own goals objectively.

What exactly do you want to happen if you are too ill to care for yourself? Who should inherit your wealth, and in what manner should it be passed along at your death? Over what time frame should the principal be distributed? If you predecease your spouse, should your documents protect your jointly acquired assets up to that time for the benefit of your existing children should your spouse decide to re-marry? Are you concerned that your values are not what you see in your children and/or grandchildren? Is it your desire that your estate pay the minimum taxes necessary? At the end of this chapter I include several questions, which you should be asking yourself. Review these before your plan is documented by the attorney. The financial professional you work with can help you to address many of these questions and answer them. It takes teamwork to complete a good plan, and this is part of the effort you will need to honestly put forth.

7) Failure to prepare your children and assess their financial abilities.

When we work with our clients, we want to informally engage in conversation that will help us understand their relationship with the children. How much information about your finances and distribution wishes do you really want your children to know? Perhaps, you would like us to help in passing along only general information so they have an idea of what their responsibility will be when the estate passes. Understand that privacy can be maintained through the line of descendants if your planning is well structured.

It is important to recognize that your children may not have developed the same maturity with money as you have; nor have they lived through the same economic times. Ask yourself, "What do I need to and want to tell my children?" How well have they learned that money is a responsibility, and the greater the assets, the larger and more significant the responsibility? It is a compelling possibility that through communications with our children, we all might recover some of the same financial self-discipline of our grandparents and their parents. It is unfortunate that, in the real world, most inheritances are spent entirely within the first couple years of receipt. Can your heirs handle a lump sum disbursement; or should a plan of distribution be designed over a period of time, in the hope that their maturity in managing money will be developed given time and experience? Have your advisors met your children? They should get to know each other, at least informally, if not in a businesslike manner.

Developing wealth is gratifying; but passing it on can be treacherous. Determine what your estate is likely to be and give considerable care to the future direction of your assets. Take time out now to test the waters, and view honestly the ability of your children to understand your objectives and how they should be fulfilled. If they do not understand what it is you would want to do with your legacy, know that they most likely cannot follow up as you would have liked them to. Take the time to prepare them in advance to carry out your wishes. Determine what timing is or isn't premature for this type of process to take place with your children. Understand that if your children are in their 40s and 50s, they are usually willing and capable of hearing what you have to say.

From My Clients' Files:

"We are opening up finally. For the first time, my husband and I are talking about money. We have different views, but what's really fun, is we respect each other and we are going to work everything out. We may each need to compromise, but we will certainly know where we stand, as will our children know that our legacy, was just that, "their father's and mine to give."

As we said earlier, "The art of preserving lifestyle and assets is through the use of communication." Communication can be specific or general. It may be difficult to talk about prolonged illness, incapacity, or death between spouses and with children. However, it is only after these issues are addressed that everyone feels more comfortable. It is when you are already in the situation that these issues are too difficult to discuss and are only moderately attended to.

13

Living Trusts Are the Answer

"Most people live in the cobwebs of whether or not to have a living trust."

Popularity has gained in the area of living trusts, and no wonder. Today people are more educated in Estate Planning. Through the sources presently available, knowledgeable people make good decisions—decisions which are well informed and timely.

The question we address in this chapter is not whether you should have a living trust, but when. Many of the old clichés of financial and estate planning never did work. For example, when a person had the ambition to develop assets, they were first told to have enough life insurance and money in the bank. A story I remember well is my father's own experience. He had one hundred dollars to invest. He called a broker and the broker abruptly hung up on him. If he had been discouraged, he might never have become a successful investor. These old clichés, many of them passed down by the large banks and insurance companies, have little basis for good judgment. Issues dealing with our financial circumstances are constantly in momentum. If you are one of those persons dwelling in the cobwebs of whether or not to have a living trust, understand that this question has already been answered for most people. The only question is when.

You will pursue the opportunities available by setting up your trust when you are willing to commit the time, and relatively insignificant fees necessary to create a plan. Your efforts in these initial stages of planning will save hours of costly administration and unnecessary publicity at the time your estate is distributed. Equally important is that you and your spouse will have peace of mind knowing that you have provided for the risks of living too long. This discussion follows in Chapter 14 where I will go into more detail on the subject of incompetence and disability planning, and is also covered in WHAT IS A PERSON'S "RIGHT TO DIE" AND IS A LIVING WILL NECESSARY? by Sherri Hynden in Part III.

The initial estate planning solution, Stage I Planning, must properly coordinate your living trusts, pour-over wills, durable powers of attorney, living wills, and health care surrogate designations. This is quite a mouthful, but with careful and professional guidance, you will know that you are wise to plan to offset most risks ahead of time. To support and clarify the general information in this chapter, you should research, read, and pursue all information via print and seek competent estate planning professionals. They are readily available and capable of assisting you. A good place to start is the local library and by calling the Estate Planning Council in your area.

Who you choose to coordinate your living trust will determine the benefits derived. How much you understand what you need to do, and the execution of your decisions relies heavily on the professional you work with. Living trusts encompass a technical area but are a dynamic solution to the ever-increasing tax burdens and lifetime risks in managing assets. Initially, the tax planning available is limited to protecting your unified credit from Federal Estate Taxation upon the first spouse to die. However, it is possible Uncle Sam may be your beneficiary only to the extent you desire.

Informally, the revocable living trust is what I term "a person entity." It is taxed the same as you are individually. Your social security number now becomes your federal ID# for the trust. If today you hold a stock certificate titled "John Doe," then tomorrow under the trust, you will hold your certificate titled as "John Doe, trustee, for the John Doe Trust U/A/D (under agreement dated) 00/00/00." Your assets continue to be your responsibility, and the personal or professional management of these assets need not be interrupted. A living trust is private and flexible.

The titling of assets under the trust name allows continuity of asset management and cash flow. If you have made the mistake of holding assets separately, then you are exposed to the impossibility of managing your assets during disability or incompetency. If your assets such as real estate, are held jointly and require your signature to dispose of, you are forcing a freeze on these assets during a time when you are incapable of handling financial decisions or signing a legal document.

A properly funded living trust can eliminate the costs and hassles of probate or guardianship proceedings, at your disability. If you are disabled, your affairs continue to be taken care of in a prescribed manner. You remain in complete control of your assets for as long as you desire. If you choose to engage an outside investment manager or trustee, this service becomes more readily available through the use of a trust. The trustee holds, manages, and distributes the property for the benefit of the beneficiaries named in the trust.

As creator of the trust, you and your spouse may also be the beneficiary(s). You may receive all the income and whatever amounts of principal you choose. You may amend the trust during your lifetime if you choose to. The distinguishing and elegant feature of the living trust is the creation and operation of the trust during the lifetime of the grantor. This is contrasted with a testamentary trust created under the provisions of your last will, and placed into operation only at your death.

A revocable living trust is the key to avoiding the complexity and confusion of settling the estate passed via a will with its incorporating delays, petitions, inventories, bonds, and fees. The necessary services of maintaining custody of the assets, collecting and depositing income, making timely purchases and sales, redeeming bonds, and keeping records can be performed by your successor trustee at death. During your lifetime, you may be named the trustee, or another individual, two or more persons, a bank, or similar fiduciary institution.

A revocable living trust is as the name implies revocable. It may be amended or revoked by the creator of the trust at anytime. However, in naming a successor trustee at death, the provisions under the document now become set according to the creator's wishes. You can take pleasure in knowing that privately, and without interruption, your legacy may continue on through your trust, or be distributed outright to your descendants. By continuing the management of your assets under trust until your heirs are capable of handling it, you are protecting them against unscrupulous persons, as well as their own possible improvidence. The trust can provide a central vehicle for professional management of assets for the support, health, education, and benefit of surviving family members, thereby avoiding possible disturbances in their lifestyles and requirements.

There is specific information you must provide to your estate consultant in order to effectively draft your documents. Some of the questions you will need to address are the following:

Who is the settlor or grantor?

You are the settlor, the creator, the grantor. You are the person who creates the trust and for whom it exists during your lifetime.

Who is the trustee(s)?

The trustee is the person who manages the assets according to the language in your document. You will most likely be your own trustee (self trustee), where state law permits. You will continue to manage your assets in trust in the same manner you are managing them today. You now make investments as the trustee in the name of the trust. An exception to a self trustee program would be if you chose to name a commercial trust company, bank, or another individual as sole trustee or co-trustee.

Who will be the successor trustee?

A successor trustee steps up at your death or disability to handle the management and/or distribution of the trust assets according to your specific wishes as documented in the trust instrument. The successor may be a spouse, a child or children, a trusted family member, a trusted and capable friend or advisor, a commercial trust company, or a bank trust department. There may be a provision in your document for the removal of a trustee by the majority vote of the beneficiaries, and/or the right to name a new trustee if dissatisfaction occurs with the existing trustee (trustee removal clause). A successor trustee also preserves the right to step down as trustee if he or she is unable to perform the duties required of them.

Who will be the beneficiaries?

You will be the first beneficiary of the trust assets and income. Ultimately, you will need to pass your legacies to the persons, or entities you name. Perhaps you wish to divide your estate equally among your children, or perhaps you wish to provide specific shares to your grandchildren and children. If you include your grandchildren, be sure to read WILL MY GRANDCHILDREN PAY A GENERATION SKIPPING TAX AND CAN AVOIDANCE BE ACCOMPLISHED THROUGH PROPER PLANNING by Andrew J. Krause in Part III of this book. The estate tax liability may increase because you have improperly prepared for skipping a generation in your estate distribution plan. It is possible to have a combined tax erosion of 85 percent of the estate if GST considerations are not taken into account when leaving legacies to grandchildren. Be sure to name specific bequests to other persons and charities if these are to be included in your plan. Provide for a "catch all" if your beneficiaries are not around to receive their inheritance. For example, will the assets go to their family, or revert back to the surviving brothers and sisters?

What manner should you use for the timing of distributions to your heirs?

Often, my clients express a concern for their children's capability to handle a large sum of cash and assets at the parents' passing. Think about this extensively as it applies to your own situation. As we discussed in an earlier chapter, know your childrens' capabilities to handle money. Experimenting with financial responsibility during your lifetime may be a way of monitoring and developing the adult child's maturing nature to dealing both with the emotional and financial wisdom needed at the passing of your legacy. If a child is handicapped, you may desire to continue the trust for their lifetime with streams of income only, or income and principal at the trustee's discretion as needed or warranted. A spendthrift provision can be written into the trust which may protect the childrens' inheritance from claims by creditors: If your children are involved in litigation, then their share may be protected for their benefit under the properly drafted document. Consider whether you would like to distribute income only with some sort of timing schedule for the distribution of principal. An example would be 30 percent of the trust assets at age 25, 30 percent at 30, 30 percent at 35, with the remaining capital distributed at age 40. A trust can do almost anything you feel you would like to accomplish in the passing of your legacy.

Will your trust create two separate trusts at your death?

If your assets were to exceed $600,000, including future appreciation, then you will want to include language in your document that will separate your unified credit by depositing assets of equal value to the unified credit exclusion available into the "Family Trust" at your death. This trust may continue for the optional benefit of your spouse during his or her lifetime and later is distributed to the remaining beneficiaries.

It works like this:
During your lifetime one trust then
"The John Doe Trust" at death divides into:

TRUST 1—FAMILY TRUST	TRUST 2—MARITAL TRUST
All income to spouse Principal for: Health, Education Maintenance, Support $5,000 or 5% of trust valuation for miscellaneous reasons	**All income to spouse** All principal to spouse for whatever reasons Full value includable in his or her estate at death
At surviving spouse's death to children	**At spouse's death** remainder to children
No estate taxes due	**Estate taxes paid**

At the death of the surviving spouse, the Family Trust passes to the heirs free and clear of Federal Estate taxes regardless of the value at this time. This trust is essentially treated as its own non-taxable entity for Federal Estate tax purposes.

The assets in the Marital Trust are included in the survivor's estate and taxed according to his or her tax rate. Historically, there has been a unified credit amount that is exempt from taxation.

If an estate is significantly over $1,200,000, the spouse may wish to disclaim his or her income interest in the family trust, permitting the assets to appreciate. The marital trust may be used to take care of living expenses. The assets that accumulate in the family trust will pass tax free on the federal level, regardless of their value. This provides an exceptional tool to pass on appreciating assets at the time of the surviving spouses death, free and clear of estate taxes.

What questions should you ask before you have your trusts drafted?

Primarily, this is the type of questioning that needs analyzing and serious consideration must be given to the character, financial abilities, and needs of your spouse and your children. Consider taxation and whether or not you have taken advantage of tax shelter opportunities to reduce the combined total family income taxes during your lifetime and estate taxes after your death.

Have you properly assessed the liquidity needed at the time of death? Should assets be reallocated to provide a simplified equal distribution, especially where a family business may be involved? Have you had a conference with all your advisors to work out an over all integrated estate plan? Have you determined how your assets should be managed, and what restrictions or flexibility the successor trustee should have?

Do you have any minor children, and if so, has a proper guardian been named? Have you obtained maximum income and estate tax benefits in any charitable program you may have? If you have business interests, shall they be continued or sold at your death? Have you taken steps to minimize excise taxes that may be due on your pension and qualified plan? Does your estate plan contain provisions to minimize the devastating but possible effects of the Generation Skipping Tax (GST tax)? Have you made an inventory of all your assets and how they are titled? Does someone know where this information is? Are you or your spouse citizens of a foreign country? Who will be your personal representative and/or executor of your will? Do you and your spouse have an executed will/trust? Are you the beneficiary of an irrevocable trust or revocable trust now in existence?

Do you have a premarital or post-marital agreement? Are you expecting an inheritance? Have you previously filed any gift tax returns? Do you have assets located in a state other than your state of domicile? Have you considered what custom design your trust may need to handle specific family situations?

Once the trust is executed, how do you retitle your assets?

Once you have determined which assets should be held under your trust, the asset must actually be retitled in the trust name. This avoids probate as the asset never passes through the will at your death. In effect, the trust replaces the will for distributing that particular asset ultimately to the heirs. The control over the asset remains the same during your lifetime. Instead of signing your name, you sign your name as trustee. Any sale, exchange, or buying of these assets is done by you or the individual or company named as trustee for the trust. Proper titling (we call this "funding the trust") would generally work as follows:

Securities (Stocks and Bonds)

If your securities are held under a brokerage account, the accounts themselves can be simply funded into the trust. This is accomplished by setting up a new account in the name of the trust, with a letter of instructions and a copy of the first page and signature page of your living trusts. The brokerage firm may also require a copy of the trustees duties as outlined in the trust, or a "certificate of trust" may be provided. The broker will then internally transfer the positions held in your name alone, to your name as trustee.

If you hold a stock or bond certificate in your name, then a proper transfer letter with supporting documentation must be sent to the respective transfer agent. (The agent is listed on the face of the security.) Mail your request and the original certificate along with a stock power to have the certificate retitled by way of registered mail, return receipt requested. Allow 4 to 8 weeks to receive a newly retitled stock or bond certificate back in the name of the trust. I would suggest you go through your broker where the retitling is usually a matter of servicing your account.

Real Estate

Your attorney should be the one to assist you in preparing the proper retitling documents for each property you own. Each deed must be processed in the appropriate county courthouse. For out-of-state property, this procedure can be cumbersome. A new deed is issued and sent to you, properly documented in that county. Most trust attorneys will include the retitling of your primary and secondary residence in their trust fees, but will ask that you pay the proper recording stamps and nominal retitling costs for additional properties. In some states, it may be wise to leave your personal residences outside the trust. Consult your attorney on these matters prior to changing your deeds.

Mutual Funds

A letter of instructions, signature guaranteed, along with a copy of your last statement, and supporting documents that the trust has been created, will inform the fund family to retitle your account in trust name. This is not considered a sale or exchange for income tax purposes. Your social security number remains the same, except if an investment held in your spouse's name is now being retitled into your trust. Be specific as to the new titling on the account, and complete a W-9 under the trust name for withholding information required by the mutual fund. Some mutual funds will require additional paperwork and will send this direct to you for final execution.

Pension and IRA Accounts

In most every case, your pension and IRA accounts should be left outside of your trust. These type of accounts allow for a direct beneficiary to be named, thereby avoiding the probate process. Your spouse, for income tax planning purposes, should be named as primary beneficiary. Your contingent beneficiary should be changed to read the name of the trust, if this reflects your objectives.

Bank Accounts

You will need to open a new account under the trust name. You have the option of showing this designation on your checks, or leaving it off, however the signature cards should always be signed as "trustee." The bank will require a copy of the trust document for their files. Be sure to change your certificates of deposit, money markets, and savings accounts. Your attorney may recommend you maintain a checking account in individual names for purposes of annual exclusion gifts.

Insurance and Annuities

The way you set up your estate plan determines the ownership titling and beneficiary designation of any insurance/annuity programs you own. Insurance avoids probate as long as you do not name "your estate" as the beneficiary, so it is not necessary to change ownership. You may wish to designate the trust depending on your distribution wishes and income tax planning options. Most insurance companies provide their own forms that must be signed, notarized, and sent in to effect a change. Very often, life insurance plans maintained to help provide liquidity to the estate are assigned to an irrevocable trust. This type of trust will be discussed in a later chapter.

The living trust is a tool to protect and carry on your legacy, privately. There is no probate; no public record of who you pass your assets to. It is unfortunate, but there are some people in our society who thrive on grieving spouses and uneducated, but suddenly wealthy heirs. Plan to avoid subjecting your family to an unpleasant circumstance where a lesson in handling financial matters may be hard learned.

Consulting a professional who you feel comfortable with and have a high level of confidence in may be equally important to your heirs as well. Your consultants can support the family's involvement concerning the acceptance of your legacy, and be a strong shoulder to lean on when needed.

Each main clause in your trust provides a certain power to the grantor, trustee, or the beneficiary. The trust can be outlined as follows in a very generic manner:

General Trust Outline

Introduction

Date Trust Agreement entered into, parties named as settlors, parties named as trustees, county & state of residence

I. Rights reserved and granted by settlors
   a. Additions to the trust
   b. Amendment and revocation
II. Dispositive provisions during the settlor's life
   a. Payment of expenses
   b. Payment of income provisions
   c. Disability definition
III. Dispositive provisions at death of one settlor
   a. Payment of funeral expenses and other items
   b. Income and principal to surviving settlor
IV. Dispositive provisions at death of surviving settlor
   a. Termination or continuance provisions of trusts
   b. Payment of funeral expenses or other items
   c. Distribution of trust to beneficiaries as designated
V. Powers of Trustee
   a. General powers including the following:
      1. Power of Sale
      2. Power of Lease
      3. Power to loan and invest
      4. Power to manage securities
      5. Power to hold securities in the name of a nominee
      6. Power to insure
      7. Power to borrow money and hypothecate trust assets

    b. Power to retain trust property
    c. Investment powers
    d. Power to determine principal and income
    e. Payment to minors and incompetent beneficiaries
    f. Power to compromise claims
    g. Distribution or division in kind
    h. Payment of taxes (death, gift, and other)
VI. Special Provisions of the Trust
    a. Spendthrift provision for beneficiaries
    b. Resignation of co-trustees
    c. Naming of successor trustees
VII. Execution of the Trust Document
    a. Signature page
      1. Settlor executing trust
      2. Acceptance of trustee(s)
      3. Witnesses
      4. Notary
    b. Each page of trust initialed by settlor(s)

Transferring your assets into the trust name is the only way to make this document effective for you. If you forget to transfer something during your lifetime, then the "pour-over will" will take care of this funding at your death.

The Pour-Over Will

The pour-over will is a will generally containing little or no assets. It accepts any assets that were left outside the trust at death (a legal settlement, etc.) and "pours" them over into the trust for proper management and/or distribution. A personal representative is named in this document, and these assets are usually entered into the probate court.

The pour-over will can also contain a separate list of your tangible property, such as favorite personal assets; family jewelry, and art collections, and designates who is to receive them. This is done by making a list and signing and dating it at the bottom. From time to time you may change this list on your own.

Durable Power of Attorney

A durable power of attorney as addressed in Chapter 14, should contain a provision that allows the holder of the power to title assets in the name of the grantor's trust. This may help to eliminate assets not included in the trust should you get sick unexpectedly before the funding is complete.

From My Clients' Files:

"We looked all over, we can't find Mom's will, we have no idea what her assets are. She told us she had a trust, but we don't know what was actually completed. She has been in the hospital 36 days now and we have had a tough time trying to handle her affairs. Where do we turn to?"

When you complete your estate plan, be sure to tell your children what documents have been completed, if nothing else. *Also* share with them your advisor's names, firm, address, and telephone number and let them know that a copy of everything you have executed is on file. When proper life time planning is done, the entire family benefits from not having to waste time and can devote their attention to caring for and making decisions on your behalf.

14

Protecting the Risks of
Living Too Long

*"For the first time in history, we are
living to see our children retire."*

There are special needs and complications that exist for the over 50 age group. According to recent estimates, almost 42 million Americans are over age 60, almost 13 million are over age 75, and one of the fastest growing age groups in our population, that now numbers over 3 million, is the 85+ age group. Our book has addressed the issues of properly arranging your affairs in the passing of your estate. Yet untold, is the suffering that occurs when we go on living a long, but unhealthy or incoherent life.

One major uncertainty, whether openly discussed or not, is whether you or your spouse, a parent, or another relative, will require long-term chronic care in a nursing home, residential care facility, or special care in the home. Generally, the husband is older than the wife, is entitled to a higher private pension or social security, has more assets titled in his name, and will be the first to require comprehensive medical care if he does not predecease his wife. But let us not forget that the risks can be far more encompassing and perhaps different than we mention above. It could be possible that the wife is older and in ill health, and may be more affluent than her spouse. In either case, the devastating effect that there may not be quality of life due to health reasons, can impoverish the healthy spouse to the extent that an entire change in lifestyle must be made. The scary recognition that this change for the caretaker could happen, often prevents this type of discussion from beginning between spouses or among elderly parents and their children.

Your estate plan must include documents with provisions that will take care of you during your life time. Through sickness, incompetency, or disability, you have a right and an obligation to secure your assets and consider medical attention. Possible devices to be included in every estate plan will be living wills, durable power of attorney, health care surrogate, or appointment of a guardian or conservator in case of a future need. Each state determines the acceptance of the above, and special care must be taken to dot your i's and cross your t's. In the above documents, the attorney's advice is invaluable, and you should never attempt to design your own documents.

The court system can provide all the necessary provisions to secure your health wishes or financial decisions if you are unable to do so. If you choose to allow this by not pre-planning yourself, then be prepared. Your spouse and/or caretaker will go through tedious, time-consuming, and costly efforts to do something on your behalf. The court will first determine if your spouse is to be named your guardian. They will require constant monthly reporting and detailed records. The courts will take a long time deciding exactly what your wishes and rights are. Quite possibly, decisions will not be made in time to avoid devastation and catastrophe to the family. It was in 1989 that Florida decided to complicate the process of guardianship proceedings. The main revision of the Florida Guardianship Law was to protect against the unnecessary loss of a person's right to handle his or her own financial and health affairs. But now, tedious and costly proceedings must be followed if documents are not in place prior to a disability or incompetency. Check the laws in your state of residency. If you have not planned adequately to avoid guardianship provisions, now is the time to. Reference the article How Do We Decide and Prepare for Custodian and Guardianship Appointments? by Joseph B. Cox, Esquire for a well-written summary on this topic.

Are you willing to put in the time now so that your loved ones are prepared to handle medical responsibilities on your behalf if the need arises? If you were in an accident which resulted in serious medical conditions and were about to close a real estate sale where your signature was required, neither your wife, nor your fiduciary, or your child, could sign on your behalf unless you specifically, under correct and valid form, preauthorized them to do so.

There are only a few terms to familiarize yourself with in the realm of risk that exists when medical complications formalize:

The Living Will

Check to see if your state accepts the "Right to Die" or "Living Will." This document, if valid, directs health care providers that it is your desire that no extraordinary life support means be used in terminal situations where death is eminent. Your health care providers are protected, under the law, from civil or criminal liability for following your wishes. Sherri Hynden follows the details that arise in her article discussing living wills, WHAT IS A PERSON'S "RIGHT TO DIE" AND IS A LIVING WILL NECESSARY? If you are concerned with this area of prolonged life through artificial means then read her article and follow up with your attorney. Most states have very specific language that must be included and dictate how the document must be executed and put in force. Please make your family physician aware you have signed a Living Will by providing him or her with an executed copy.

A competent adult may also name a "Health Care Surrogate" which is a person who, on your behalf, may make health care decisions. This would include officially naming your spouse with the authority to apply for medical benefits and consent to medical procedures, if you are incapable of decisive action or consent. Your designated health care surrogate only steps in when two of your physicians conclude that you cannot make your own decisions or provide informed consent. Your attorney will need to know who will have the right to make these decisions for you. If your spouse is named first, perhaps a contingent person will be your oldest child. Naming an alternative should eliminate the need for any amendments if your spouse is unable to act for you given medical complications. I do not suggest that you complete a Living Will and designate your health care surrogate on your own or through a mass marketed document, but seek the work of a competent attorney.

Durable Power of Attorney

I have never met a person who wishes to give up the management of his or her affairs. Regardless of how you fit in with the rest of us, you should be assured that everything is taken care of if an "alternative manager" must be named in your place. A perfect likeliness to not having a power of attorney in place would be having the IRS participate as an unwritten beneficiary in your estate plan. The courts will get involved in your day to day affairs unless you specifically write them out. The Living Will, Living Trust, Durable Power of Attorney, and designation of a health care surrogate are just a few examples of keeping your life within your given and authorized control. A Durable Power of Attorney can support your wishes. The power authorizes another person to manage your affairs in your absence or incapacity. The "durable" power permits this authorization whether or not you are capable yourself. In the state of Florida, durable powers can be given to any person, related or non-related. If someone other than your spouse is designated, then notice to the spouse must be made. If there is no living spouse, then the adult children should be notified of the person holding the power. When you talk with your attorney, keep in mind the type of decisions that may need to be made on your behalf in the future, even if they are not relevant today. Your power holder should be given authority to arrange for and consent to medical procedures and to fund assets into your living trust, along with normal provisions such as:

1. To receive, demand, collect, and obtain possession of any and all manner of debts, notes, mortgages, claims, choices in action, obligations, or monies due or belonging to you; and any of the same to compound, compromise or settle; and releases, discharges, receipts, or acknowledgments therefore to execute and deliver.

2. To sign, execute, endorse, deliver, or pay any and all checks or drafts; to make, enter into and perform agreements, contracts, or any other instruments in writing of whatever kind that said attorney may deem proper.

3. To pay any and all debts, claims, or obligations incurred by you or by your attorney for you, for which you or your property may be liable.

4. To deposit or withdraw any money or credits in any bank or savings and loan company or any depository or investment or financial business of any kind, and to sign, endorse, execute, or renew any checks, withdrawals, deposits, promissory notes, bonds, bills of exchange, or evidences of indebtedness and to waive notice of demand and protest and to transact and perform any and all other banking or financial business and affairs of any kind whatsoever.

5. To effect insurance upon the life or health of any person or upon any property, real or personal, and to rescind, cancel, or collect

the proceeds for any insurance, including life, health or accident, and to compromise with releases or discharge, any insurers of claim against any insurers or claim against any insurer. In connection with any life insurance policy (including annuity contracts) and any health insurance policy in which you may have any interest, to demand and receive all amounts payable and benefits of any kind, to exercise rights and options, and to surrender such policies. You hereby relieve and release all such insurance or other companies making any payment or payments to your attorney or at your attorney's discretion, in connection with the exercise by your attorney of any such privilege or benefits, of any and all responsibility.

6. To purchase, sell, transfer, assign, hypothecate, redeem, exchange, waive priority, or deal in any other way with any notes, mortgages, stocks, bonds, or securities or investments of any kind or nature whatsoever, and to receive and receipt for any and all income or dividends therefrom and to vote or to execute proxies for voting any and all stock.

7. To borrow money upon the security of any property, real or personal, and to execute and deliver promissory notes with mortgages or liens upon any real or personal property to secure the indebtedness upon such terms as said attorney shall believe best.

8. To lease, rent, release, manage, deal with, purchase, sell, contract to purchase or sell, and convey in fee simple or lesser estate by deed or any instrument, and the same to deliver with or without covenants of warranty for such price and upon such terms of credit, and with such other provisions, and to such person or persons as my attorney shall deem proper, the whole or any part of or any interest in any lands, tenements, hereditaments or any personal property, tangible or intangible, of any kind whatsoever and wheresoever situated; and to preserve, repair or improve any such interest or property as said attorney shall deem proper.

9. To make, execute, and file any and all tax returns upon personal or real estate, income, or any other tax that may be levied or imposed by any lawful authority, and to settle, compromise, or pay the same or to collect any and all refunds or repayments thereof.

10. To invest and reinvest in any kind of property, real or personal, without regard to any statute or rule of law concerning the investment of funds held by fiduciaries.
11. To have access to any safe deposit box standing in my name alone or jointly with another or others.
12. To vote stock, give proxies, and participate in any plan of corporate reorganization.
13. To bring and defend actions in law or equity and to compromise claims.
14. Without prejudice to the generality of the powers otherwise granted herein and conferred upon said attorney, the specific power is hereby granted to redeem and receive the payment upon, assign and transfer, sell, endorse, deliver, and exchange, and have reissued in coupon, registered or any other form, any securities of the United States, including, but not limited to treasury notes and treasury bonds of any kind, denomination or date whatsoever, owned by the undersigned or in which the undersigned has any interest or title of any kind, and to receive and receipt therefore or for any such reissued or substituted securities, and to do and perform any other act or thing with respect to any securities.
15. Take all steps and remedies necessary and proper for the conduct and management of my business affairs.
16. Do anything regarding my estate, property and affairs that I could do myself.

The Medicare Catastrophic Coverage Act

The current Medicaid Laws are a combination of federal and state programs which basically provide medical care to the needy. The provisions of the law were created under MCAA, (The Medicare Catastrophic Coverage Act) in 1988, of which the Medicare portions were repealed in 1989 leaving the Medicaid portions that became effective in most states as of October 1990. This area of providing medical care is perhaps one of the most serious problems we face today, with concerns increasing in our future. Think of the longevity of our parents and grandparents due to medical advancement and the devastating effect of rising health care costs. It is possible that sickness or accident could cause serious erosion of sufficient assets and income. Being familiar with Medicaid laws and benefits may become a very time-consuming, confusing, but important issue in your family.

All states must cover nursing home care but they can each determine, with some flexibility from the federal guidelines, the extent to which the medical needy will be eligible, and the amount of income and assets that determine "needy."

Medicaid issues are constantly addressing lifetime transfers and protecting your spouse against impoverishment. It is not out of line to guess that monthly health care facility costs can run between $3,000 to $5,000 a month. Under your own circumstances, could your spouse continue to provide for his or her own health care if you needed constant medical care for any length of time? Familiarize yourself with the "look back period" that determines how much in assets and income you may have to qualify for Medicaid assistance, looking back to see if any transfers were made to exclude assets from your estate. A certain flat monthly income is permitted, with some exceptions. If your pension is above the state specified limit, and you need care that is more costly than what your cash flow provides, you still may be disqualified from receiving Medicaid assistance.

The best way of being prepared for a medical catastrophe is to

1. expect it as life expectancy tables increase;
2. have adequate insurance coverage;
3. have more than sufficient assets to provide the care that you are accustomed to receiving; and
4. seek advice from counsel where a healthy spouse is involved to properly set up your planning documents and the entitlement of your assets.

Spouses, children, and parents should discuss their legal obligation to provide support for a medically needy member of the family. Be sure that impoverishment of healthy family members is not a consequence of your planning. Take steps now to avoid the risks that occur from living too long, and take the steps necessary to ensure the quality of life you and your loved ones deserve.

You may have already signed a living trust to provide for asset management during periods of incapacity, that can also avoid probate in the estate settlement process. But to fully complete your plan, work with your attorney to include the living will, the pour-over will, the health care surrogate, and durable powers of attorney. If your children are to step up in place of your spouse, then be sure you discuss, at minimum, the generalities of these solutions and the choices you have made. We, as financial professionals, can appropriately serve to facilitate discussions within the family when needed.

From My Clients' Files:

"I want to know that I will never be a financial burden to my children. It is equally important how I feel about certain issues, and what is important in handling my affairs and what is not."

Naming contingent parties on your additional estate planning agreements is an area where it is very possible your children may become involved during your lifetime. This has little to do with how you are set up financially. Talk with your children, give them a copy of your health care surrogate and living wills as well as a copy to your doctors, and explain to them how you feel. Discussing these issues openly and honestly leaves room for a healthy environment to exist between family members when catastrophe strikes.

15

Preserving Assets
through
Family Gifting

"Gifts are a blessing from the government;
learn to make your gifts wisely."

We have thus far covered the basic, but very important, first steps of proper estate planning. For the family whose estate is in excess of $600,000 or $1,200,000 total between husband and wife, further tools for defusing the taxes need to be discussed. If you aim only at foiling the federal government and not paying one cent in gift or estates taxes, the remedy is at hand. Simply leave everything to charities. Our tax laws concerning lifetime gifts and leaving legacies puts no ceiling on the deduction allowed for charitable gifts and bequests. Charitable planning is discussed in Chapter 16, however, most people want to know how the tax can be alleviated or reduced while incorporating their family members as the major benefactors. I'll proceed now in talking about gifts for the benefit of family members, other than spouses, for which the marital deduction also puts no limits on gifts between husband and wife as discussed in Chapter 11.

Few people recognize that the federal government does limit the amount of gifts we can make to our children gift tax free. Three exceptions exist to this tax law. You may give unlimited amounts to an educational or medical facility directly on behalf of children, grand-children, sisters, brothers, or whomever else you decide to include in your generosity. The second exemption is the unified credit that allows us to offset federal estate tax or gift taxes due on up to $600,000 of bequests or lifetime gifts. This exempt amount can be used during your lifetime to make a direct gift outright to your children or to a trust for their benefit. When you're considering making a significant gift of up to $600,000, several factors have to be addressed. First, the cardinal rule is "Take care of yourself first." Be sure you are financially and emotionally capable of transferring $600,000, or if husband and wife join together, up to $1.2 million out of your control, and subsequently out of your taxable estate. There are also ways to gift through the use of trust, that can provide some peace of mind that your children are not unfairly expected to have the proper maturity to manage this amount of money and will not squander it before your very eyes.

There are advantages for those who can afford the flexibility and privilege of utilizing their $600,000 exempt amount during their life-time. Not only will you remove this capital from possible taxation, you will also remove any future appreciation these assets may have from being includable and thus taxed in your estate. This leverage is very valuable for significantly sized estates.

The third exempt provision is the use of your allowable annual gift exclusion. This annual opportunity says you can hand out up to $10,000 to anyone you choose, once during each calendar year. This gift is in addition to your $600,000 credit or medical or education payments. With gift splitting by spouses, you can actually give $20,000 to each and any number of children, grandchildren, etc. Gifts or gift taxes are not deductible for income tax purposes (unless contributed to a quali-fied charity).

If a gift exceeds the exempt annual exclusion, then a gift tax is due and payable by the bestower of the gift or the grantor. In a situation where a taxable gift occurs, a return must be filed by April 15 of the year following the excess gift. Your advisor can help you with all these details. There are meaningful reasons why, if your estate is over $3 million—$9 million+, you may want to make taxable gifts beyond your $10,000 annual and $600,000 one time exclusion. The complex-ity of this topic leads me to ask that you speak directly to your advisory group on this. The details are beyond the scope of our book.

When you make a gift of assets other than cash and marketable securities, the question of value comes into play. This is a difficult area especially when it pertains to gifts of closely held stock in a family business. If you estimate, for example, that 10 shares of stock are equal to $20,000 in value, and give away these shares to your daughter, be sure you can back up your valuation. The $20,000 would be within your annual exclusion provided your spouse joins in the gift. However, the IRS could come back later and argue that the value was really $35,000. In this case, if they win, then the $15,000 must be applied to you or your spouse's unified credit, if still available. If the $600,000 was previously used, then the $15,000 is subject to gift taxes payable by the person effecting the gift. In either case, because it is a gift, it is not subject to income taxes.

It is important to remember that in many ways, the support we wish to give or not give to our children, is controlled by federal and state tax laws. If you give to your children $10,000 for their birthdays, you have used up your allowable gift for each child for the calendar year. Incredible! This means that you cannot give them anything more for Christmas. In reality, most of us are concerned with giving too much to our children in that we might destroy some of the value they place on their own ability to generate income and build an estate. For these reasons, we try to understand the family situation and financial circumstances as they exist. If reduction of taxes in the parent's estate *is important,* then perhaps a gift program can be established that will not actually pass to the children or grandchildren until much later, perhaps even after your deaths. This is where trusts apply. Just a few more points to cover before we get into the Irrevocable Trust Plan.

By following a consistent program of annual lifetime gifts to your family, you as the estate owner, can *dramatically* reduce the size of your taxable estate. The following chart should help to illustrate the results of such a gifting program. The assumptions are based on an 8 percent growth rate of these gifts, outside your estate. For example:

Assume you are a single spouse and have five children, you may gift up to $50,000 per calendar year ($10,000 to each child).

If the Annual Gift Is:	The Value of Your Gift For the Number of Years Over Which the Gifts are Made Is:			
	5 Years	*10 Years*	*20 Years*	*25 Years*
$50,000	316,796	782,274	2,471,146	3,947,721
If you are married and your spouse joins in:				
$100,000	633,593	1,564,549	4,942,292	7,895,442

Marginal Estate Tax Brackets

Estates Up To	Top Bracket	Estates Up To	Top Bracket
$600,000	No Tax	$1,500,000	45%
$750,000	39%	$2,000,000	49%
$1,000,000	41%	$2,500,000	53%
$3,000,000	55%	$10,000,000	55%

Using the above chart, if you were the single parent, had a gross estate of $1,500,000, and made $10,000 gifts annually to each of your children for 10 years, the savings benefits to your legacy would be:

A		B		C (Savings)
$782,274	×	45%	=	$352,023

If you were married, had an estate of over $3,000,000, and used your total annual exclusions available of up to $100,000 for your five children over 20 years, the benefit would be:

A		B		C (Savings)
$4,942,292	×	55%	=	$2,718,261

To calculate your savings, plug the numbers that apply to you into this formula:

A = Potential amount removed from your estate
B = The estimated top tax bracket percentage
C = The amount of tax savings which would pass to your heirs

Perhaps you don't have 20 years to make these gifts and reduce your estate, or it is impractical, or not financially sound to transfer your total available annual exclusions from your estate. In this case, consider the use of life insurance. Life insurance used alone, or combined with other assets in your gift plan, and properly removed from your estate, provides a potential wealth building and wealth preservation effect that becomes very dramatic. Gifts made within three years of death are not considered in the computation of the taxable estate. It is important to note though, that gifts that exceed the annual exclusion may be added to the taxable estate as "adjusted taxable gifts." This, in effect, pushes the remaining assets into a higher tax bracket, but the icing on the cake is that all the appreciation on these assets from the date of the gift until the date of death is not brought back into the computation.

The only exception to the above is gifts of in-force life insurance policies made within three years of death. Certain incomplete transfers (for example, revocable transfers where you do not give up the right to the assets, and retained life estates, or GRITS where death occurs before the end of the term) will also be included in the gross estate without regard to when they were made. These areas apply to advanced and more complicated measures of trying to keep your legacy intact. Instead of covering these technical and specialty areas, we will concentrate this chapter on one of the most rewarding straight forward estate planning tools that can be used by most everyone: the Irrevocable Trust or Supertrust, or Wealth Replacement Trust Plan (the later is covered in Chapter 16). In particular, when an estate reaches $2.5 million it enters the 55 percent tax bracket.

When 55 percent of each additional dollar of estate growth is "earmarked" for estate taxes, many estate owners look for methods of *freezing the growth* of their present estate. We have touched on one of the three techniques used over the years when we explained gifts of assets. Areas too detailed to cover here also include intrafamily sales of assets (installment sale, private annuity), and changes in business organizations (corporate recapitalization, personal holding companies, and multi-tier family partnerships).

The advantages of making gifts during your lifetime can multiply depending on the structured program you use. Just a few advantages include:

1. Transferring future appreciation out of your estate.
2. Paying gift taxes from the taxable estate in most cases if they are due.
3. Reducing current grantor income taxes by removing assets that previously cash flowed taxable income.
4. Avoiding probate administration on gifts made during your lifetime. If gifted directly, you as the donor can see the beneficiaries enjoy the assets while you are still living. If gifted in a trust combined with life insurance, we can experience the magnified effect of otherwise smaller gifts.

Properly planned, you can creatively organize today's affairs to avoid pitfalls and enjoy the opportunities that exist for passing on your legacies (assets and values) tomorrow. A proper estate and financial plan cooperatively managed helps you to embrace the present and face the future with confidence.

For the highly successful individual, or family, no means exist under current law, to transfer large amounts of wealth and provide financial security, that are as certain or as dramatic as the Irrevocable Life Insurance Trust. Incredible federal estate and state death tax savings are possible through an irrevocable trust which has as one of it assets a life insurance policy on the life(s) of the grantor(s).

The Life Insurance Trust

Since estate taxes are imposed upon the capital assets of your estate, most of our clients prefer to pay taxes with capital of the estate, and not from current income.

By utilizing proper gifting methods, you may transfer capital to a trust designed to hold as one of its assets, life insurance. The benefits ultimately distributed from the trust are substantially increased. This increase is a result of the "balloon" effect of life insurance, and the escape from taxes on these assets, both estate and in most cases, income taxes. Leveraging life insurance through tax savings under a trust can bypass you and your spouse's estates and substantially increase the amount effectively passed on to your heirs. You may also avoid state death taxes. The irrevocability of the insurance trust protects these assets from claims by creditors. There will be no probate expenses, delays, or uncertainties with respect to the distribution of the assets held by the trust. The grantor, who in most cases is one of the insureds on the policy held in the trust, has more control over the ultimate distribution of the proceeds than he or she would have in making an outright gift to the heirs. This control is established at the time of writing the trust and prior to execution. Once the document is signed, the grantor relinquishes control over changing the provisions under the trust. Some benefit is allowed when rights are given to a third party for limited changes, for example, should the tax law be altered causing necessary changes to be made under the document to keep it current.

There are two basic ways to create an irrevocable insurance trust:

1. You make an absolute assignment of one or more existing life insurance policies. Under this type of setup, it is advisable to review the "three year rule" that includes the proceeds of the insurance contract back in the taxable estate if the insured dies within three years after the transfer. Additionally, old policies should be reviewed for their credibility as to whether they should be maintained or should be replaced with a more modern contract.

2. The trust may be established first, then cash contributions are made by the grantor. Under this method, the trustee actually applies for and secures the policy on the life or lives of the insured(s). There is no "incidence of ownership" by the insured that confirms the escape of the proceeds from being subject to inclusion under the grantor/insured's estate.

The trust may be funded or unfunded. A funded trust has income-producing assets transferred to it that are used to make the required yearly deposits to the insurance company. Typically, most irrevocable insurance trusts are unfunded, and the grantor assumes the responsibility of making proper gifts to the trust so that the trustee may maintain the policy.

The excellent use of "crummey powers," which allows the money going into the trust to be construed as a "present interest gift" is what allows the much larger future death benefit proceeds to be exempt from estate taxes. The technique is many times referred to as the "Crummey Provision" after the case that decided the validity of this technique, *Crummey v. US, 397 F.2d (CA-9, 1968)*. Use an attorney who is familiar and well-versed in drafting these types of present interest trusts. The Local Estate Planning Council in your area can refer you to attorneys that specialize in this area. Since you, as grantor, are making a gift to the trust, and not directly to your beneficiaries, the trust will allow the beneficiaries a "limited power to withdraw" certain sums from the trust for a short time after your contribution is made. Although it is not anticipated that a child will exercise his or her power to withdraw, this gives the beneficiaries a "present interest" in the gift.

Through the use of proper technical language, we effectively can have a trust with no adverse gift tax consequences.

Because insurance proceeds are often used as a prime source of liquidity for estate taxes and expenses, it is important to return this source of liquidity for the insured's estate. This can be accomplished under several methods, primarily, the trustee can be granted the discretion to make the proceeds available to the estate, either by way of purchasing assets for their fair market value, and/or making loans to the estate. This valuable tool can prevent a "forced sale" of a business, real estate, or securities portfolio, and keep specific valuable property in the family. In effect, the assets are exchanged between the irrevocable trust and the estate. The powers granted the trustee must be discretionary. If your trust document directs the trustee to pay debts and estate taxes with the policy proceeds, these funds will be pulled back into your estate and be taxed.

What are some of the areas of designing this type of plan that will need to be understood prior to entering into such an advanced estate plan?

There are always costs, though limited here, to entering into an Insurance Trust program. First, you must give up the use and enjoyment of assets you use to place into the trust. This can allow for a minimum change in your cash flow picture. Once you name the beneficiaries, you have no right to change or add to the trust beneficiaries. You do, however, have the right to initially state in the document who is to receive what, and in what manner it will be distributed (outright, overtime, income-only, and principal to bypass children's estates and go on to grandchildren if desired). There will be attorney's fees to set up the trust, which will be insignificant when compared to the benefits your legacy will gain.

The trust is required to have an identification number even though no tax returns are required if no income is generated. To accomplish this, a non-interest bearing account can be established to accept the gifts prior to funding the life insurance plan. This account is titled in trust name and allows for ease of management and bookkeeping. The trustee is the signer on the account and can draft a check for the planned premiums to the insurance company. The insured/grantor should not pay the premiums directly to the company.

A unique way of increasing the tax leverage that may be gained in an irrevocable trust is to have the document set up as a "Grantor Trust." If income is generated, the grantor is responsible for the income taxes. Paying income taxes is not considered part of the annual exclusion used to transfer assets to the trust. In a way, additional benefits are passed to your children. Remember, the trustee may purchase investment assets as well as life insurance. This makes for a "Mega Trust" concept.

In most cases, survivorship insurance, insuring the lives of both spouses and paying out on the survivor's death, or second spouse to die, is used to fund these types of trusts. This provides for liquidity and distribution at the time when the rest of the legacy is passed on to your heirs and the federal estate taxes will be due.

When the objectives are to provide benefits, first, to a surviving spouse, and then to children, a single insured is used, and the spouse is granted certain income benefits under the law.

When the goal is to pass the trust assets when the rest of the legacy is passed on, who would be named as trustee?

The answer to this question requires a great deal of thought because the trust is irrevocable once established. The insured should in no case be named as the trustee because he or she may be deemed to have incidence of ownership over the policy proceeds: only under specific circumstances should the spouse be named and only if he or she is not also the insured. Consult your legal counsel for more on this area. A family member, for example, one or more of your children, may be named as trustee. During your lifetimes, there is very little to manage if only insurance is held under the Trust. If you include other assets, an investment adviser may be named to offer guidance to the individual trustee(s) on the management of the assets. An individual may not charge a fee and as a beneficiary they may have a more personal interest or special expertise in managing the trust affairs (i.e., managing the family business exchanged to a trust designed to carry on after both parents' deaths).

Don't forget, though, to consider the benefits of a corporate fiduciary. They don't die or become disabled; therefore, "permanence and trust" are established. They are financially accountable for their mistakes and they can be a non-biased party to the many beneficiaries involved. This may prevent any bitter attitudes toward an individual friend or relative serving as trustee. Corporate fiduciaries have investment expertise, tax and accounting liabilities, computer capabilities, and keep current on the constant changes in tax laws. It is possible to give the beneficiaries co-trustee powers or the power to remove and name another corporate fiduciary. This power to change trustees or work more closely with a financial adviser is recommended in most trusts, and can help to keep everyone on the proper path.

Who will be your beneficiary under the Irrevocable Insurance Trusts?

For each beneficiary you name, you are entitled to use up to $10,000 of your annual exclusion to effect transfers to the trust. With your spouse joining in, up to $20,000/year/beneficiary may be removed from your taxable estate and sheltered under the Irrevocable Trust. Be careful when including children's spouses as it is unfortunate today that many marriages can end in divorce. It is okay (and in the large estates recommended) to use grandchildren as ultimate possible heirs. For instance, your children may be given the right to use trust assets during their lifetime, and live on the income generated, or accumulate assets in the trust that will bypass their taxable estate as well and be distributed estate tax free to their children (your grandchildren). This is known as planning for Generation Skipping Privileges. Be sure to ask your advisers how this can benefit you given the size and nature of your assets and basic estate plans.

It is impossible for us to find an estate planning tool or technique that under current law can match the properly arranged irrevocable life insurance trust, in terms of providing significant financial security for your survivors at such a minimal tax and other cost.

"Properly arranged" means that this area of planning requires more than average competence on the part of the drafting attorney, the estate/financial adviser, and the trustee. It takes teamwork to get it done right.

"Irrevocability" means just that. Once the transfer is made to a trust, the property cannot be easily, if at all, recovered. Of course, life insurance is not an asset generally needed by the grantor and our goal is to remove these assets from your taxable estate when the proceeds become significant (when the policy pays off at death).

"Cost" is related to gains. The life insurance trust properly completed is one of the most cost-effective means of transferring large amounts of wealth. However, it is not "free" and, as always, good tax planning is beneficial only when employed as part of the result in accomplishing your "non-tax" goals. If you have an estate increasing in value, you must take the time now to study these techniques.

From My Clients' Files:

"When Dad died, the IRS valued our inheritance, which included the business, at 20 times greater than we knew it was worth. The tax was $854,000. We could not pay it and we were forced to liquidate assets to settle the estate. I was 52 at the time and this was my livelihood. I will take the time to make sure my own planning will not leave my family with the burden of changing their lifestyle when it's my time to go."

One sad circumstance in planning is when the need and desire for setting up an insurance trust is evident by the parents, but neither spouse is insurable. Under this scenario we are forced to go to more costly and less effective alternative plans. Even sadder, though, is when there is the insurability, but the time is not taken to set up a proper Irrevocable Trust Strategy. The choices at distribution are limited and the heirs are forced to react instead of pro-act. A non-decision is many times related to confusion. Lucky for most that though Insurance Trusts are technical and sophisticated tools to reduce tax exposure, much information and case law can allow for relative ease in educating yourself. Decide then to implement this strategy as one of your favored tools to pass on the legacy you worked so hard to create.

16

Making Sense
of Your
Charitable Intentions

*"Charitable planning is a smart way to be a
philanthropist and pass wealth to your heirs
free of gift and estate taxes."*

Great cultural facilities have been built, medical research advanced,
our environment improved, skills taught so handicapped people may
lead more balanced lives, educational opportunities made available,
and many life encompassing quests accomplished, because of our
attitudes toward building a better tomorrow.

Charities play a major role in enhancing our future and our children's
future. No donation, small and token, or large and significant, goes
unnoticed by a non-profit organization who counts on our support to
carry on its mission. Your eagerness to incorporate charitable gifts in
your planning is important to them.

Generally, a gift is made because of charitable intention, not necessarily to save taxes. However, once you have decided to contribute,
plan your gift for maximum personal and family tax benefits. When
you have decided the approximate value of the legacy or current gift
you wish to leave to charity, your next decision lies in answering these
questions: "What kind of asset should I use for my gift?"; "When
should I effect the gift; at death via a bequest, or today when I am here
to be a part of the charity's progression?"; "How do I complete the
transfer and where should it go, to multiple charities or one favorite

charity?". These may sound like relatively simple questions, but considering all the possibilities to put you one step closer to planning for tax reduction and amplified benefits for your family and the charity(s) is very important.

Among the choice of gifts that can be made, you will either allocate income over a period of years, or gift principal assets, such as highly appreciated securities or other property, or gift cash. Whether your charitable intention should be carried out during your lifetime as opposed to a bequest at your death, requires careful consideration. Charitable Trusts that are set up properly during your lifetime can bypass probate and the hassles and costs that may be associated with settling the estate. Current gift planning can permit immediate and effective transfers to charity at your death.

Support for non-profit organizations comes from various sources: individual bequests, foundations, and corporations. Individual bequests are responsible for over 50 percent of monies raised to benefit charity. For purposes of this chapter, we will concentrate on ways to benefit from "individual" donations.

Gifts may be made outright or in trust. Our tax laws encourage us to make contributions to charitable organizations. We have the government's blessing. Taxpayers who file an itemized return benefit personally by receiving a deduction against federal income taxes for making the gift. This savings in taxes is an effective way to reduce the out of pocket cost for the gift actually donated, and other related costs to gift giving programs.

For example, if you gift $1,000 in cash, and you are in a 31 percent tax bracket, then your net out-of-pocket gift is $690 ($1,000—$310 tax savings). Charitable gifts, no matter how large they may be, are exempt from gift and estate taxation, and do not use up any of your unified credit or count towards your annual gift exclusion rights.

When cash is given, our government permits charitable deductions up to 50 percent of your adjusted gross income. If your deduction exceeds this amount, the excess deduction can be carried over to the next year and used against AGI under the same 50 percent rule. This excess deduction carryover can only be used for up to five years.

Let's assume for example, you make a donation of $100,000 cash and have an adjusted gross income of $50,000, your deductible amount this year is $25,000 (50 percent of AGI). You may carry forward $75,000 of unused deductions. The following year you may use up to

50 percent of AGI, and so on, until the full deduction is used up or five years has passed.

Gifts may be made from cash, appreciated securities, or real estate, appreciated art works, antiques, or other tangible personal or investment property.

Cash Gifts

If your intentions are such that the charity have immediate use, cash or assets convertible to cash can be used. Giving cash is generally not the most viable method to enhance the benefits that can be available for the charity or the donor. Appropriate time should be given to learning about additional planning that can be done to enhance the final results of giving.

Appreciated Securities and Real Estate

There are circumstances where selling a security and gifting the proceeds to charity can make sense. Perhaps you need a tax loss to use against capital gains from other holdings. For example, a stock you bought for $10,000 is now worth $6,000. You sell it, use the $4,000 loss on your return and gift $6,000 in cash to charity. You may then deduct the $6,000 as a cash gift on your return using the 50 percent rules discussed above.

However, it can be tax wise to contribute a security directly to the charity if it has appreciated in value. The donor receives additional benefits, a deduction based on the present fair market value of the asset, and avoidance of the capital gain tax that would otherwise be due on the ultimate sale of this asset.

These types of gifts generally have a ceiling on deductibility of 30 percent of your adjusted gross income (AGI) with the same five-year carry forward rule. The appreciation on the gift was considered in the calculations for the alternative minimum tax (AMT) calculation at one time. The new tax laws changed this provision and we no longer have to be concerned about the effect of a charitable gift of an appreciated asset on AMT tax calculations.

If appreciated assets are held short term (less than six months), then the deduction is limited to the cost basis. Still, no tax is due on the appreciation and this follows the 50 percent rule as if you had given cash.

Gifts of Appreciated Works, Antiques, and Other Gifts of Tangible Personal Property

Almost any type of asset may be given to support a charitable cause. The value used to calculate your deduction is based on whether or not the gift relates to one that may be used for the charity's exempt function. Will the gift you make be used directly for the purpose of the charity? An example would be gifting a painting to a public museum. The deduction here is 30 percent of AGI on the value of the gift. If you were donating a piece of furniture to a charity that presents cultural events, most likely this gift will be auctioned off to raise money to support the charity's purpose. A tax benefit is still available, but the deduction is for the asset's cost basis only. Property held long term is 30 percent deductible, whereas property held short term is 50 percent.

When working toward developing a charitable plan, hire and coordinate a professional team that understands the technicalities involved. They should be able to provide proper creative planning advice specifically for you and run the illustrations and tax calculations that are necessary prior to setting up a charitable gift plan.

Gifts of Life Insurance

A gifting program that includes life insurance not only enhances your philanthropic intention, but yields substantial tax savings as well. There are several ways insurance may be incorporated: (1) gifting an unneeded policy, or (2) using life insurance to replace the value to the family for a significant gift made to charity, or (3) amplifying a gift that can be used by charity in the future to support a more significant need.

When gifting a paid-up policy, the gift value must be determined by the replacement cost of this plan. Deductions on a gift of life insurance are limited to the policy's cost basis. You can determine this by summing up the total premiums paid, less any benefit received (cash withdrawals, dividends). A life insurance gift requires a change of ownership and beneficiary, effectively removing the proceeds from the insured's estate.

If your policy requires more premiums after the gift is made, know that this, in itself, provides additional tax deductions for each deposit you make. If you choose not to continue tax deductible premium payments, then the charity must choose from the policy options available. They may choose to continue the premiums so the full face value will be recognized eventually, or perhaps elect a paid up policy for a reduced face value amount, or cash it in for the full surrender cash value.

Today's modern life insurance also provides tremendous opportunity in that it allows the philanthropist to magnify his or her gift. An example would be a husband and wife who have determined their financial and philanthropic choices are to make a $5,000/year donation to the charity, for a minimum of 10 years. With this goal in mind, they may qualify to take out a joint and survivorship insurance plan with a face value of perhaps $500,000. The charity is named the owner, and their total intentions of gifting $50,000 have enhanced the value of their gift to charity. What a wonderful contribution this would be to your favorite charity's endowment fund. Additional funds of $450,000 are available to support the objectives of the charity, and add to the continuity of the charity within the community and a better tomorrow.

Gifts of different assets as described above may be given during your lifetime or by a bequest through your will or your estate plan at death. When waiting until your death to effect a gift, you lose valuable income tax deductions and the value of knowing how the charity has benefitted. However, gifts at death do create a deduction against the taxable estate for federal estate tax purposes.

Life Insurance may help your favorite charity in a much different way than described above. Should you desire during your lifetime to make a gift outright or in trust, from assets otherwise includable in your estate, life insurance can be used to fund a Wealth Replacement Trust. This type of trust funded with life insurance creates a vehicle to provide assets to your family that replace the value of the gift that went to the charity. You'll realize multiple benefits and carry out creative and exciting philanthropic intentions by opening your mind to a new world of tax and estate planning for charitable giving using life insurance and trusts. This technique is popular among grantors who wish to pass their legacy on to their heirs intact. The wealth replacement trust is not includable in their taxable estate. Cash flow may be generated from your charitable gift if effected through an appropriate trust tool. This additional cash flow can provide the dollars necessary to fund the wealth replacement trust.

Using Charitable Trusts

Your gift during your lifetime may be made outright or through the use of trusts. If you choose to retain part of the asset, this can be accomplished through a trust.

A trust set up for charitable purposes is an "irrevocable" trust. Once designed, it may not be revoked. You may, however, retain the right to name different qualified charities, designate trustees, and add new gifts in future years. You may, in some cases, be the trustee of the charitable trust. Options are almost unlimited as to how to set up your trust, what kind of trust, should the charity manage the trust, or should a separate management relationship be set up all together. Trusts create an opportunity to split benefits between yourself or family members, and the charity. Two interests are created under the trust. Who gets each interest is determined by the type of trust you create.

Charitable Remainder Trust

Under the Charitable Remainder Trust, the donor continues to receive income, and the remainder in the trust at the donor's or surviving spouse's death passes to the charity. Additionally, as the donor, you receive a current income tax deduction to be used to offset taxable income on your tax return. It works like this:

There are two interests that are created:

Income Interest	Remainder Interest
You and Your Spouse	Your Favorite Charity(s)

There are two types of charitable remainder trusts you will find most commonly used. The Charitable Remainder Annuity Trust is set up to pay a stated income amount for the life of the trust. This type of trust is typically used when as donor, you want "guaranteed" cash flow each year, and the assets you will hold in the trust are not expected to appreciate in value.

For example:

You make a gift of municipal bonds assuming the face amount is $1,000,000 with a yield of 6.5 percent and you are currently receiving $65,000/year cash flow. When the gift is made, and we determine the annuity trust will be for 6.50 percent income interest, the municipals were worth $1,127,000 because of current market appreciation. The lifetime income you receive will be $73,255.

A more commonly used trust is the Charitable Remainder Unitrust. This trust is set up to pay a stated percentage of the value of the trust, either monthly, quarterly, semi-annually, or annually. Typically, highly appreciated assets are placed in the trust, and if the assets are sold to diversify the portfolio, generally investments would be made that might be expected to grow in value over time. Remember, the charity can sell the asset and pay no taxes for the capital gains recognized.

An example of charitable planning using a CRUT (Charitable Remainder Unitrust) could work well within the framework of your own financial, tax, and estate planning endeavors. Assume for a moment that you own 1000 shares of XYZ stock which is currently worth $500,000. Your cost basis on this stock is $100,000. You are unhappy with the 2 percent yield and wish you could make the asset more productive for cash flow purposes, yet you're cautious against doing any form of a sale because your taxes will go up. Another concern is that this stock is a significant part of your portfolio and is too heavily weighed in one area instead of well diversified . You are a bit uncomfortable with what the company is doing now. We have calculated that a sale would cost you $140,000 in capital gains taxes, leaving only a net to invest of $360,000. If invested at 7.50 percent your income would be $27,000. Oh we forgot, your income tax rate is 31 percent, so your net income would actually be $27,000 less $8,370 or $18,630. This is an increase from the $15,000 in dividend yield you were getting, but your capital was reduced by capital gains taxes you had to pay. Perhaps there could be a better way through entering the world of charitable giving, a more sophisticated technique to gift, but retain more.

Taking the same example as Mr. and Mrs. Gift above, we instead gift the entire 1000 shares of stock to a CRUT. We state in the set up of the trust document that this trust will pay us 7.50 percent of the value of the assets held, not less than yearly, regardless of whether the asset produced 7.50 percent income. In years following this is what could happen hypothetically:

Year 1

Proceeds to trust equal $500,000, -0- taxes are due, and 7.50% is paid to you or $37,500 that year assuming the gift was made January 1st. This was an increase of $22,500 over your otherwise $15,000 dividend. (If taxed at 31% your net cash flow would equal $25,875.)

Year 2
We assume that in year 2 your trust is holding only 500 shares of XYZ stock, and the other half was sold and reinvested. Zero (0) income taxes were due. The trust investments gained in value for a total valuation of $543,000. This year's calculation requires the trust to pay you as donor, or your surviving spouse, 7.50% of the $543,000 or $40,725.

Year 3
Just as assets under your own portfolio can fluctuate in value, especially where equities are used, so can the trust. This year the value went down some and the trust is worth $527,000 for a total of $39,525 payable to you this year.

These examples attempt to make you aware of some key considerations. The trustee can be directed in the document to invest in different forms of securities or fixed accounts, pretty much like you would do on your own. Because of the CRUT nature, you can participate in either appreciation or depreciation of these assets through an increase or decrease of your income.

OK. We've taken care of you. You are happy, your assets are better diversified, and you are receiving more income, but what about that legacy you wanted to leave to your children? $500,000 is gone from your estate. We could use some of the increase in cash flow to fund deposits necessary to carry a life insurance plan on both spouses lives. This contract can replace the value of the asset. However, exactly what is the worth of these assets if they had passed to the children? Assume you are in a federal estate tax rate of 50 percent. If you left the asset (1000 shares of XYZ stock) to pass outright the net value after taxes is $250,000. Insure the $250,000 or the full value of $500,000. The choice is yours to make. This insurance should be held under The Wealth Replacement Trust so that no federal estate taxes are due at death.

The Wealth Replacement Trust
This vehicle works very similar to the Irrevocable Trust or Supertrust Plan we described earlier. In the example above, the couple chose to fund the trust with $4,500 yearly for 10 years for a total insurance

benefit purchased by the trustee of $500,000. The plan was set up as a Survivorship plan; therefore the insurance pays only after the surviving spouse passes away. The same type of distribution wording may be used as in most other trust documents. Even Generation Skipping provisions can be set up to enhance the benefits of your planning. (If you have a significant size estate, be sure to ask your advisors all about GST planning using irrevocable trusts coupled with insurance and other investments if feasible!) The net effect for the couple I describe above was:

1. They received an additional $18,000 in cash flow each year after the Wealth Replacement Trust was funded.
2. They will be satisfied in knowing they have made a significant gift to their favorite charity(s).
3. The children will receive 2 times their normal inheritance because the legacy they left is protected from the Federal Tax bite because this legacy was developed inside the trust.
4. They received a current income tax deduction for the future gift they will leave to the charity(s).

From My Clients' Files:

"I know we spent many hours to get the trust set up and determine which asset would be gifted. The fun part was knowing I left my children more, I benefitted by receiving additional cash flow, and I am more than pleased that when I go, my children and my church will have received a part of my legacy."

I have found that properly and effectively presented, most people with significant assets, especially where they have had appreciation, enjoy the tools available through a well-thought out charitable gift plan that encompasses a Wealth Replacement Trust. Even if you are not Charitably inclined, it can be worth your time to review these ideas. If you are gifting to charity now or through a bequest in your will, ask your advisor how you can set up a win-win-win plan. The charity, the children, and you may all benefit. Happy Gifting!

17

A Challenging Discussion about a Boring Subject

"The world of insurance has become a specialty of technical professionals. No longer can we work with just a good salesman and expect to receive a plan that will continually be properly serviced."

Life insurance is a necessary and important factor in our planning, even considering the unpopularity and distaste for addressing this subject. Insurance is more a philosophy than a product. Some of you choose to use it; some choose to let the government take what it wants and then let the children get what's left over.

The use of life insurance, when not mistreated or misrepresented, can add a vital and distinctly favorable result to your estate plan. Life insurance is a way to create, preserve, or help distribute your legacy in a simple and tax-favored way.

We talked about insurance when incorporating gifting programs to set up an Irrevocable Trust or Supertrust. We also touched on this subject when we addressed the Wealth Replacement Trust used in conjunction with charitable planning. The most significant question we face now is how to incorporate life insurance in our planning— "What company? What product design? What insurance consultant to work with? How do I properly fund the plan? Will the policy hold up if interest rates or dividend scales are reduced? Do I use a joint and survivorship plan? A joint first to die program? A single life plan? Universal life? Whole life? Term? A combination? How much is too much or too little?" "I'm confused" is the general response you will have should you direct yourself on this course. You will want to give the insurance program as much consideration and time as you give to setting up and executing the trust documents. You must work with a professional who is a technician not just a well-trained salesperson.

Buying insurance today is not what it used to be, even as recently as 10 years ago. It's only been the last few years that insurance agents, insurance companies, and clients alike have recognized the mass revolution that has taken place in the whole of the insurance industry.

In this chapter, I'll only address life insurance as it relates to passing on your legacies. There are other reasons you might utilize insurance, and there are other types of insurance you may need to address. Talk with your health and casualty, flood, or medicare agent about your needs to look at these other forms of insurance.

Insurance of yesterday took on very basic characteristics. You either purchased term (group or individual), or whole life (from a stock or mutual company). The product in most cases required continuous premiums to be paid during your lifetime, and there was a guaranteed interest rate credited to your policy value. It was in 1977 that the first variable life insurance plan was introduced. It has only been in the last couple years that it has gained popularity. Up until this time the investment portion of an insurance contract (cash value) was invested in the general portfolio of the life insurance company (consisting mostly of long-term bonds and mortgages). More about this later.

It was in 1979 and the early 1980s that "universal life insurance" was introduced. This creative new product came into being by the demand of the consumer to participate in the high interest rates being offered at that time. A mass exodus of cash values from life policies began through loan provisions directed to high yielding money markets and CDs at the banks. The life companies were forced to respond. This evaluation of universal life has changed the insurance industry. These changes benefit us, but they are confusing—confusing because too many choices are given and too much of the burden now lies on the consumer and the professional to design a program that will stay in force and do its job, the way they expect it to do. Hence, the beginning of a new business, one that centers around highly technical and competent insurance specialists.

Universal life was the beginning of account statements that showed the distinction between mortality and expense charges, and the cash value part that was credited with an additional interest rate over and beyond the guaranteed rate offered for the life of the contract. Different from the fixed premium, fixed cash values, and fixed death benefit of traditional whole life, universal life offered more flexibility. With a competitive and properly designed universal life plan, total flexibility can be given to design and redesign the death benefit, the premium, and the cash values. At the very minimum, expense and mortality costs must be covered by either excess cash value or premiums paid. The most that you can deposit into a universal plan or modern whole life plan (single premium whole life or interest sensitive whole life), is controlled by the Internal Revenue Code in Section 7702 that was introduced in 1988. I'll discuss the income tax ramifications of life insurance in just a moment.

The mid-80s, with major revisions in the early 90s, introduced the next step to life insurance; the universal variable life insurance program. The flexibility of a universal life plan is offered, along with choices as to how the cash value of the policy is invested. Sub-accounts are set up that resemble "mutual funds" as we know them today.

Term insurance is a type of insurance that most of us are familiar with. In the realm of using insurance to cover calculated risks, term can work. But in the breadth and depth of an advanced estate plan, true term insurance is difficult to accept. Perhaps the reason is due to the "limited coverage period" that term policies provide. When used in an Irrevocable Trust for estate planning purposes, you want the life contract to be in force even if you are 80+ or 90+ years old when you die. This generally is when you need the benefit to be paid!

There have been a number of hybrid policies that came into play in more recent years. The choices have certainly multiplied.

The most factual statement I can make about our discussion on life insurance is, "It would be very wise for you not to start with settled preconceptions when addressing the use of life insurance." Careful consideration is necessary for each alternative that is presented. Understand that all types of insurance have a cost. *Nothing comes for free. Even these smaller portions.*

Many of you have heard of single premium whole life insurance. This product's birth was in the early '80s and allowed for a one-time maximum cash payment and very minimal life coverage. This enriched the "investment benefits" of the contract. The benefits since 1988 have been modified and now may be a good time to address the income tax consequences of owning life insurance. First, and most important, the "ballooned benefit" of the proceeds payable at death are free from income taxation. This favorable treatment has kept insurance lobbyist close to home on Capital Hill fighting to preserve it forever.

Whether or not early withdrawals or loans from an insurance contract during the insured's lifetime are free from income tax liability depends on how the plan is structured and your payment schedule. If the plan is considered to be "modified" then pre-distributions could be reportable for income tax purposes. Even if this is a unique and disadvantageous character of SPWL (single premium whole life), the advantages are that at death the insurance proceeds are still income tax free. Confusing? Yes. It takes careful time and attention as to what you would expect your insurance to do for you and your beneficiaries during your life and after. This is where we help. We ask numerous questions first, then design the plan, choose the company, and complete health qualifications to pick the proper program to use (see the article by Jeffrey Anderson, How Can We Understand the Funding Requirements of an Insurance Contract? for more on this).

Insurance benefits can be paid in many different ways. These are a part of the "optional settlements provision" in your policy contract versus a lump sum payout. However, with the advent of trusts being used today as the key document that does the planning, the insurance contract generally pays in a single sum to the trust for further distributions according to specific document language.

Life insurance almost always is paid out income tax free. This is marvelous! (The only exception may be under the transfer for value rule too detailed to cover here. If you are transferring an existing plan, speak with your professional team on this matter before proceeding.)

Though you may understand the income tax free benefits, many of you do not know that life insurance proceeds are includable in your estate if you own the policy, or have any incidents of ownership in the policy. What does this mean to you? Let us review an example. Perhaps a widow, Mrs. Life, has an estate of $500,000 and a $250,000 insurance policy. She dies thinking the children owe no taxes. Wrong. Her estate is worth $750,000 total and taxes will be due on the $150,000 of insurance that places her estate above the $600,000 currently exempt amount. No matter who the benefit is payable to, it will be taxed. This is the reason sophisticated clients set up special trusts to own insurance, which puts it out of the estate. Now we see the light; no income taxes and no estate taxes, what a benefit to families suffering the turmoil of how to distribute their legacy on to the next generation intact!

We could talk about many areas in life insurance but we would be defeating the purpose of our book, which is to keep it simple and stimulate you to act, to move forward in your own planning. In closing, I have some key pointers: 1) do not rely on hypothetical illustrations using current rates of return available in the market. Be conservative—look at what makes the contract tick at different earnings levels and varying premium payments. It is unfortunate, but the industry has learned to mislead through these proposals, (in many cases the agent was not taught any differently). Instead the proposal should be encouraging more depth of understanding as to how these contracts work; 2) work with a technician who is part of your professional team, who understands the relationship of your financial planning, and your estate planning, to the management of your insurance program. Remember, earlier I said insurance was a philosophy as well as a product; 3) your plan must be continually managed, and reviewed for changes in tax laws, mortality costs, contract expenses, changes in premium funding, and changes in economic factors just to name a few; and 4) work with a company who is positioned to be solvent and competitive (see Louis Clementi's article, HOW DO WE BEGIN TO ANALYZE THE INSURANCE INDUSTRY WITH RESPECT TO A PARTICULAR COMPANY AND PRODUCT TYPE?).

This is the last chapter in Part II and I just have a few additional comments to share with you. I hope we have helped you to know how important it is for you to develop and complete your plan. Why risk it any other way? I wish I could share so much more with you. This is a frustration I always carry. It is so important, these issues we address. How does your planning differ if a second marriage is involved, what if a large part of your estate is made up of retirement plans (IRAs, pensions, profit sharing plans, Keoghs, 401K)? How does it work if the bulk of the assets are subject to taxation? Does your family business, that has grown in valuation, have little or no liquidity to cover the taxes that would be due? What if your major asset is a summer home that you want to stay in the family, should you set up a

GRIT (Grantor Retained Income Trust) to pass this asset more favorably under the current laws in effect?

So many special considerations. My only problem is I don't know who *you are* and this is really where we have to begin. Your estate plan is uniquely developed and custom fitted during your lifetime.

From My Clients' Files:

"I am so relieved at how much we have accomplished. Now I can go back to enjoying that which I do best. Golf! Fish! Tennis! Swim! Be with my family and feel my affairs are all in order."

Begin today. Don't procrastinate! Life is much too valuable!

PART III

Observations & Advice from the Professionals

For Part III, we have picked out some of the estate planning questions often asked. The awareness and observations are furnished by financial professionals who have proven their knowledge, commitment, and concern on behalf of their clients.

The answers by these contributing authors will give you confidence in dealing with your own financial advisors.

Don't put it off . . .

18

How Can We Understand the Funding Requirements of an Insurance Contract?

by Jeffrey L. Anderson

Mr. Jeffrey Anderson is President of Flexible Planning Corporation, a firm that specializes in distributing insurance products to independent financial planners, insurance agents, and other financial professionals with regard to clients' estate and other planning needs. Although Mr. Anderson managed the Western New York area for a New York State insurance agency for two years, he is a 25-year native of Naples, Florida. Jeff is a Series 7 licensed representative and is affiliated with FSC Securities Corporation. Mr. Anderson also provides technical support to financial professionals, and serves as an associate affiliate for Ciccarelli Advisory Services, Inc.

Life insurance as a means of preserving estate taxes is one of the most useful tools left to preserve one's estate. This generally applies to people age 55 or older. This is when estate planning awareness becomes a significant issue in a person's financial retirement.

The concept is this: you pay premiums to an insurance company; they promise to pay your heirs a cash benefit upon your and/or your spouse's demise. The theory being, that you give them less than they ultimately give your heirs. This is called leveraging your gifts.

But how much will it cost? The creative funding and design of insurance contracts today gives you considerable flexibility and control over a life insurance policy. This can be an advantage as long as there is a complete understanding of how the contract is priced, and if the terms of the contract (i.e., guarantees and assumptions) are favorable to you. Unfortunately, many premiums are calculated using unrealistic and/or misleading projections. Many contracts afford the insurance company considerable flexibility in making changes on existing and new contracts. It is important that you understand the difference between projections and guarantees. Projections are what the company "expects" to happen. Guarantees are the worse case scenarios. In many cases, the "projections" of early funding of a life insurance policy are not sufficient to build the cash reserves necessary to keep the policy in force in later years. The result will be shock! A policyholder may be expected to make impossible contributions to keep the insurance coverage from lapsing.

It is important to understand the internal workings of the policy. The charge (risk rate) that you pay for the death benefit is reduced by the amount of cash value in the policy. The growth of cash value is related to how the contract is funded. The formula is:

$$
\begin{aligned}
&\text{Previous Cash Value} \\
&+ \text{Premiums Paid} \\
&- \text{Loads} \\
&+ \text{Interest} \\
&- \text{Risk Rates} \\
&= \text{Cash Value}
\end{aligned}
$$

To simplify, there should be a realistic and strong motivation to build cash values to reduce future mortality charges. Remember, no matter what age you were issued the contract, the older you get, the higher the risk rate. For example, a $1,000,000 insurance policy with $900,000 in cash value, results in a death benefit risk to the company of $100,000. Conversely, $1,000,000 death benefit with only $100,000 in cash value results in a death benefit risk to the company of $900,000. In the first example, you have the earnings on $900,000 in cash value to pay the risk rate charge for your attained age times $100,000. In example #2, you have the earnings on $100,000 trying to cover the charge for your attained age times $900,000. At the older ages this is impossible. In most policies there is a mortality charge table. Look up the rate for an 85 year old and multiply it times the expected death benefit. This exercise will help you understand the internal workings of a life insurance policy.

There was a day when you bought a life insurance policy, put it in the safe, and forgot it. Those days are gone. Now, life insurance contracts must be managed. It is important to work with professionals who understand this. Many life insurance policies bought today will run out of money and lapse. Working with a professional, armed with an understanding of your policy, will help you avoid these future deficiencies. Most up-to-date contracts allow you considerable flexibility to keep this from happening. However, the responsibility for acting is yours. Act while time is on your side.

Medical advancements have prolonged life and most insurance companies today look at underwriting senior citizens in a very positive way. This mature group has developed a medical history that can be reviewed by an insurance underwriter. Given a medical problem, the underwriter can see how you handled treatments, followed up doctor visits, etc. Underwriters are very concerned as to how insurance applicants follow up on a medical impairment. Do they visit the doctor regularly? Did they stop smoking? Did they follow the doctor's directions? Insurance companies have found that retired clients who are financially secure take care of themselves and have the capability to seek competent medical care. The desire to live a quality life, breeds longevity. Many insurance companies discount their guaranteed mortality charges. There can be a considerable difference in mortality charges for a smoker, which may be a good incentive to quit. By the way, if you quit smoking or your health improved since your policy was issued, your company may consider reducing your mortality charges. But you have to ask!! There is big incentive for insurance companies to keep existing policies on the books. Another good reason to work with a professional.

A well-thought-out insurance policy can be great for both living and death benefits for an estate. A poor policy can be catastrophic. Both policies can be issued by the same company.

19

Multiple Life Insurance Contracts: Are They for You?

by Ben G. Baldwin

Ben G. Baldwin is the author of The Complete Book of Insurance *(Chicago: Probus, 1994), the AICPA course on Risk Management and Insurance, and the co-author of* The Life Insurance Investment Advisor *(Probus, 1994). He is president and owner of a registered investment advisory firm, involved in financial education, consulting, and planning for corporate and individual clients. He is the originator of the "Baldwin System Financial Plan," Action Letters, Life Insurance Product Analyzer, and a computer program that determines the annual rate of return in a life insurance policy. Mr. Baldwin holds the designations of Chartered Life Underwriter (CLU), Certified Financial Planner (CFP), and Chartered Financial Consultant (ChFC). Mr. Baldwin served on the Board of Regents for the College for Financial Planning in Denver, Colorado and has taught all of the courses leading to the CFP designation.*

Survivor life insurance, Joint & Last Survivor life insurance, Second To Die, and First To Die Joint Life are all forms of providing life insurance on two lives with the death benefit being paid only at one of the deaths. The death benefit is paid at the death of the second insured with survivor life insurance, joint & last survivor and second to die but at the death of the first insured in a first to die contract (tricky names, did they give you a clue?). These policies are receiving much publicity because they require less premium than the standard life policies on a single insured. They are purported to be "cheaper." This myth has led to them being used without careful thought regarding how well they provide for specific and long-term needs.

First to Die

In the case of first to die joint life, the policies are perceived as cheap in comparison to insuring both lives under separate policies. The policies do cost less than insuring two lives because the insurance company needs to pay off only at the death of the first leaving the survivor uninsured. If this lack of insurance is a problem and the survivor is now uninsurable, or if the resources are not available to pay for what now will be a standard single life policy, then using the first to die contract has not been cheap. It was improperly used and cost dearly.

Second to Die

Second to die policies which are even more popular than the first to die are perceived as inexpensive again because people feel that they have a lot of insurance at a premium that is much less than that of two individual life policies. But again, the insurance company needs to pay off only at one death, the last of the two insureds to die. This dramatically delays the time and the chance that the insurance company will be called upon to pay a death benefit. Therefore, it is reasonable that the mortality costs, costs for life insurance within the policy, are much lower than a conventional single life policy. The "other shore" in these policies is what happens when the first of the two insureds dies. The survivor may not receive any death benefit payment and now may have to pay the premium on what is essentially a standard single life policy. Does the survivor have the resources and want to use them to service the ongoing premium requirements of such a policy? Also, what is to be the disposition of the policy if one of the insureds should no longer be one of the insureds (such as in a divorce situation, the termination of a key employee, or the breakup of a business arrangement)?

The bottom line is that these policies should not be thought of as cheap but merely policies that meet the needs of a particular situation very efficiently. Keep in mind that the very efficiency with which they provide for the particular situation is why they can become so inefficient should the situation change.

Let's take a look at some of the situations to which these policies are particularly well-suited and then give some reasons why the "cheaper" reasoning may have been a disadvantage rather than an advantage.

Situation: Husband and Wife
Need: Cash to pay federal estate tax at the second death

This is the most popular use of the second to die policy. It hits the nail on the head. A husband and wife first plan their estate with their attorney, accountant, and other appropriate professionals. This assures that their estates pass to whom they wish with a minimum of cost, delay, and complication. Having determined the most efficient method of passing their property and minimizing the costs involved, they make an informed decision not to pay any estate taxes until the second death. After estimating the inflation adjusted amount of the taxes and expenses to be paid, they buy a second to die policy sufficient to pay the estimated costs. The cash from the policy death benefit will arrive as a result of the same event that causes the taxes and expenses to become due. What could be more perfect? What possibly could make this less than a perfect decision? After all, the premium is less expensive than two individual policies and may be all the couple can possibly allocate to insurance. One of the two insureds had trouble getting insurance because of poor health, but the insurance company will accept the risk in this situation because it is based on two lives. Also the purchasers went to a number of agents and carefully bought the policy that required sufficient premium so that they did not have much term insurance that could create problems later by becoming more expensive than predicted.

What Went Wrong?

Well, here is what really happened. The couple's marriage ended in a divorce. The policy was owned by an irrevocable trust. It took some doing (time and expense) for the attorney to find that the trustee had the right to distribute that policy so that it could be divided into two policies, each for one half the original face amount and allowing each of the insureds to become the owner of his or her own policy. It was not an inexpensive or easy process because it was not anticipated or provided for in advance.

What Else Could Go Wrong?

Or, let's try this, they did not get divorced, but he did die before she did and the cost of the policy was a burden to her. The policy did not help her and she began to wonder why she should pay for it. The kids were not really being that great to her so she quit making gifts to the irrevocable trust that were necessary to pay the premiums on the policy. The mortality costs (life insurance costs) and expenses were taken from the policy values and the policy terminated leaving the trust an empty shell. At her death, Uncle Sam did take his 50 percent and the estate was destroyed as a result of lack of cash and marketability of other assets. The kids finally realized that they should have taken care of Mom . . . or figured out some way to keep the policy in force.

Another Scenario: Voluntarily Pay Estate Taxes at the First Death

Bob Hales, an attorney from California, tells a story of someone who did not buy second to die but who elected years ago to pay $90,000 of estate taxes at the first death. This allowed a piece of property to be put in a credit trust for the spouse when her husband died. The credit trust is not subject to estate taxes at the death of the surviving spouse. That piece of property was now a sizable portion of the Napa Valley. The children were not aware of the careful planning their father had done 25 years earlier and came into the lawyer's office recently with their now 90 year old mother. They were terribly concerned since they had just attended a seminar on estate taxes and were asking for his estimate of the federal estate taxes that they thought would be due on the now 36 million dollar piece of property at their mother's eventual death. The seminar leader had told them that they would owe Uncle Sam 18 million dollars but Bob told them the correct figure was zero because of the careful long-term thinking of their father (and their attorney). He enjoyed their pleased surprise immensely.

Summary

As you can see multiple life policies can be very useful but excessive use, too little premium, and poor planning can turn their advantages into disadvantages. Don't consider them the default answer to every estate planning problem.

20

When We Talk about Passing on Our Estate to Our Children, What Is the Role of the State in Which We Live?

by Stephen B. Bauer

Mr. Bauer graduated with a Bachelor of Arts degree in economics and government from Columbia College and an Master of Business Administration in accounting and taxation from the Columbia Graduate School of Business. Steve spent 23 years with one of the big eight accounting firms, the last 12 of which he served as a tax partner. He later organized his own tax consulting firm with offices in Ft. Myers, Florida and Westchester County, New York. The firm specializes primarily in tax, financial and estate planning. Mr. Bauer served as a national instructor in such areas of specialization as deferred compensation, financial planning, problems of the closely-held corporation, and mergers and acquisitions.

With the difficulties encountered in balancing state budgets, you should anticipate states making a concerted effort to tax as many assets as possible. I have found the states very aggressive in attempting to determine whether taxpayers have actually abandoned their old residences and adopted new residencies. For example, in the state of New York recently, revenue examiners visited a well-known country club and recorded the license plates of all Florida automobiles. They then proceeded to determine whether these people were filing as non-residents of the state of New York. Ironically, an individual who had some New York business interests and filed as a non-resident was much more susceptible to examination than someone who removed himself entirely from the state.

If you wish to avoid any question of residency from a former state, I strongly recommend that you sever all relationships, including notifying every company from which you receive interest or dividends of your new location, so that any form 1099 reporting will be done in your new resident state.

The question of residency plays an important role both in the income and the estate tax area. Many states have two basic tests for residency. One test is for an individual who has domiciled in his or her state. The second is for a non-domiciliary. The issue of domicile, therefore, is an essential in ascertaining whether a taxpayer is liable for tax as a resident. New York State tax has defined domicile as: "the place which an individual intends to be his permanent home/the place to which he intends to return whenever he is absent." Technically, an individual can only have one domicile, regardless of how many homes he or she may have. For tax purposes, an individual will be deemed a resident of a state such as New York and therefore, taxable on his or her world-wide income, if either one of two tests are met. Number One: He or she is considered a New York domiciliary, maintains a permanent place of abode in New York, and is physically present in the state for more than 30 days. Number Two: He or she is not considered a New York domiciliary, but maintains a permanent place of abode in the state and spends more than 183 days in the state.

Another revenue examiner informed me that maintaining ownership of one's former principal residence, in his opinion, could be the most important factor in determining whether an individual has abandoned his former domicile. For example, most taxpayers believe that obtaining a residence in Florida and spending 183 days out of New York is sufficient to avoid the New York tax. However, beware, because if the agent is successful in establishing New York domicile, and you have a place of abode in that state, then a 30-day stay during the year is sufficient to subject you to New York State taxes as a resident.

From a review of several cases and rulings, I have attempted to outline below separate items which should be taken into consideration in ascertaining whether one has established a valid domicile away from his or her former state. It should be noted that in proving that your new domicile is Florida, assuming New York was the former domicile, one single factor will be determinative but the decision will be based upon a preponderance of evidence where the burden of proof will always rest with the taxpayer.

In order to establish a Florida residency, consider the following:

- The filing of a declaration of domicile for the state of Florida.

- Obtaining a Florida's driver's license.

- Changing registration for all automobiles to Florida.

- Filing of a Florida Intangible Tax Return.

- Filing of income tax returns showing a Florida address.

- The presence within the state during substantial portions of the period in question.

- Location of the family within the state.

- Business transactions within the state.

- Relocation of bank accounts and brokerage accounts to Florida.

- Telephone and mailing address in Florida and the recital of Florida residence in any deeds and documents which are signed.

- The location of safe deposit boxes moved to Florida.

- Declaring Florida as your legal residence in the last will and testament and the retention of such will/trust in the State of Florida.

- Church and club memberships in Florida.

- If you intend to maintain club memberships in your former state of residence, change the membership to that of a non-resident.

- Registration of and actual voting in Florida.

- Ownership of your primary residence in Florida or evidence that you are building a permanent home in the state.

- Abandonment of your former place of abode, the repurchase of a residence at a substantially smaller value than the property you own in Florida.

- Filing for homestead exemption on your Florida residence.

- Notifying officials of the local municipalities and your former state of your intentions to become a Florida domiciliary.

- Registrations in hotels when you travel should be under your Florida address.

- Location of a cemetery plot in Florida.

Some revenue examiners would also look to whether the individual was originally born and educated in the state or whether he or she simply moved there for business purposes, i.e., a person born and raised in Pennsylvania moved to New York for business purposes and ultimately reestablishes residency in Florida. They may also look at whether or not any of your family members ever resided in that state and how active you were in religious or other community activities.

21

What Is the Excise Tax or "Success" Tax on My Retirement Funds, and How Can I Plan to Pay Less and Keep More?

by Paul F. Ciccarelli

Paul F. Ciccarelli has been developing and expanding financial consulting businesses with other family members from New York and Florida, including their offices in Naples, Florida. Mr. Ciccarelli majored in accounting at the University of South Florida in Tampa, and is a candidate for the designation of ChFC (Chartered Financial Consultant) from the American College. He is a certified instructor for the NCFE (National Center for Financial Education), and is a lecturer on advanced tax, investment, and estate strategies. He has published several articles on money and tax matters. Mr. Ciccarelli specializes in financial & estate solutions for individuals and business owners. He

provides technical services to attorneys, CPAs and other independent professionals involved in financial and tax consulting businesses. Mr. Ciccarelli is a member of a network of independent professionals who combine their in-depth knowledge and experience for the overall benefit of their clientele. He holds his NASD Series 7 license with a registered broker/dealer, and life insurance license.

> *"If Patrick Henry thought taxation without representation was bad, he should see how bad it is* with *representation"*
>
> *The Old Farmer's Almanac*

In the '70s, tax laws were passed to entice people into contributing money to qualified retirement plans. Those individuals who created qualified plans were offered substantial tax advantages. Contributions were tax deductible, plan assets grew tax-deferred, accumulated assets enjoyed income tax advantages on distribution, and pension assets were not subject to estate taxes at death. Congress began searching for revenue-enhancing opportunities. They saw, in the form of pension assets, a gold mine, which by 1993 would be valued at over $3 trillion. This was the birth of the 15 percent excise tax (Success Tax). I expect that this will not be the last law change effecting taxation of pension benefits.

Many of our clients have been successful at developing a considerable sum in their qualified retirement plans (i.e., IRAs, employee pension plans, Keogh plans, etc.). The Tax Reform Act of 1986 created a 15 percent excise tax (known as a success tax) on distributions from retirement plans made after December 31, 1986 which exceed certain IRS guidelines. This 15 percent "excess accumulations" tax is effective on payouts from pension, profitsharing, IRAs, HR-10s, SEPs, and even TSAs. In a nutshell, if you or your beneficiaries receive what the IRS considers too much, the excess is taxed at a 15 percent rate. The law is a complicated maze which creates a real analytical challenge for wealthy clients and their advisors in developing a retirement plan distribution formula. If you has accumulated significant assets in your pension plans, you should have an analysis completed by a professional well versed in the excise income and estate tax area. In the case of the wealthy client, the old rule of thumb —delaying distributions until age 70½—may no longer be considered sensible planning.

There are two separate tax issues involved in the analysis of the 15 percent success tax.

During Lifetime

The first issue relates to distributions the individual receives during his or her lifetime. A 15 percent excise (extra) income tax will apply to total yearly distributions in excess of $150,000, or $148,500 in 1994 for persons who elected the special grandfather provisions.*

An example of the 15 percent success tax on annual retirement plan distributions is given in Table I for both individuals who chose the

Table I

Year	Exempt Amount with Grandfather	Exempt Amount without Grandfather
1993	$144,551	$150,000
1994†	$150,333	$150,333
1995†	$156,346	$156,346
1996†	$162,600	$162,600
1997†	$169,104	$169,104
1998†	$175,868	$175,868
1999†	$182,903	$182,903
2000†	$190,219	$190,219

† Assumes exempt amount indexed at 4% each year. As long as the distribution does not exceed the exempt amount it will not be subject to the 15% "success tax."

* Grandfather Provisions—Individuals with benefits of greater than $562,500 as of August 1, 1986 had an option to "grandfather" those benefits. The "grandfather" provision effectively allowed an individual to exempt the portion of any distribution attributable to the pre-August, 1986 benefits from the 15% excise tax. In order to receive this exemption a proper election had to have been made on the individual 1987 or 1988 1040 tax return. This election was no longer available after the final 1988 individual income tax filing date (10/15/89).

grandfather by 10/15/89 and those who did not file for grandfathering.

From 1987, the IRS has increased the grandfathered indexed amount from $112,500 to $148,500. The IRS has the choice of whether to increase the index figure on a year-by-year basis.

Let us use an example of a distribution of $200,000 in 1993 for an excise tax calculation.

Distribution	$ 200,000
Less Grandfather Amount	148,500
Subject to Excise Tax	$ 51,500
Extra Tax (15%)	$ 7,725

The excise tax is in addition to $79,200 income tax at a tax rate of 39.6 percent.

Now, if you are thinking that the excise tax would only effect an individual nearing age $70\frac{1}{2}$ with a large pension, (at age $70\frac{1}{2}$ you must tax a minimum withdrawal of all qualified assets), you *may be* correct. The age $70\frac{1}{2}$ minimum withdrawal rate on a pension balance of $3,030,000 would equal $150,000 (using the joint and survivor withdrawal tables). Therefore, a pension value in excess of a $3,030,000 balance would *force* an excise tax on the excess. For most individuals, this would not cause them to lose any sleep. However, do not be lulled into comfort by this example. Congress may change the rules again relative to the excise income tax rules, and as you will see in the next chapter, there may be a greater concern for your retirement plan dollars at your death.

If an individual elects to receive a lump sum distribution (takes all retirement plan proceeds and pays income taxes), then the excise income tax will be on the amount in excess of five times the annual limit of $150,000 or $750,000; or $742,500 if grandfathering was elected.

Why would an individual choose to pay taxes on qualified pension lump sum distributions versus rolling the assets into an IRA to continue to defer taxes? There are some favorable tax options for lump sum distributions that you should be aware of, especially if you were age 50 or older on January 1, 1986. Those individuals who were 50 years of age or older on January 1, 1986 are eligible to use the 10-year averaging method or the 5-year averaging method when calculating the "regular" income tax on lump sum distribution from pension plans. The averaging method may effectively reduce the tax rate on the distribution. The 10-year forward averaging method was repealed by the Tax Reform Act of 1986 and replaced by the 5-year averaging method for individuals that were younger than age 50 on January 1, 1986.

An individual may take a lump sum distribution of $750,000 without being subject to the 15 percent excise tax. In fact, under code section 4981A(c)(4), if the lump sum distribution exemption is $750,000 and there is a $150,000 exemption for other distributions, a total of $900,000 would appear to be the exemption in one year.

Table II examines how the tax may apply to a lump sum distribution.

Table II

1994 Lump Sum Distribution	$1,000,000
Grandfather Exemption	742,500
Amount Subject to Excise	$ 257,500
Income Tax	15%
Income Excise Tax	$ 38,625

(Extra, over and above normal or averaging income tax)

Now, moving on to the second, and foremost of our retired clients, the more critical issue . . . the 15 percent estate excise tax on retirement plan distributions at death. Were it not for this second issue, the first issue (income excise tax) with the proper distribution planning, would not be an issue at all for most clients. (As long as the IRS continues to index—increase—the exempt amount in the future).

At Death

If an individual dies before receiving his or her entire retirement benefits, (or a good portion of it), an estate excise tax of 15 percent may be imposed on the amount over the IRS defined limits. The exemption for the "Estate" excise tax is more complex than the "Income" excise tax. In essence, the longer you live the less the exemption may be, and therefore, a greater amount of your pension may be subject to the estate excise tax (see Table IV, page 143).

Formula:

Total Present Value of All Plans: $ _____

Less: Present value of an annuity   _____
payable for the life expectancy of
the individual immediately before
his or her death with annual
payments the greater of $150,000
or $112,500 (as adjusted for inflation
to $148,500 in 1994) if the grand-
fathering election was made
(see Table V for present value table).

Equals: Excess Retirement Accumulation   _____

Multiplied by the tax rate × 15%   _____

Excess Accumulation Tax $ _____

This tax is in addition to the federal estate tax which has a top tax rate, as of 1994, of 55 percent (or 60 percent if subject to the 5 percent surcharge on estates over $10,000,000) and could, therefore, equate to a 75 percent total tax, or greater on the value of your pension at death. In addition, the beneficiaries, (if other than the spouse) will be taxed on the distribution (less the federal estate attributable to it) at 36 percent (or higher) federal income tax rate plus state inheritance and income taxes. These taxes may effectively eliminate most of one's heirs' benefits.

The excise tax may be deferred *if the surviving spouse is the beneficiary of all plans* (except a di minimus amount of 1 percent) and elects to defer the tax by a form attached to the estate tax return. The surviving spouse may roll the assets into an IRA. This deferral would not be available if plan benefits are payable to children or even a typical Unified Credit Trust. And, while the estate excise tax paid reduces the estate for purposes of calculating the "regular" estate tax, it should be noted that the estate excise tax may be payable even if there is not a federal estate tax, due to the use of the unified credit, unlimited

Table III

Yr. End	Age	Pension/ IRA Balance	Estate Taxes/ Excise	Estate Taxes/ Regular	Income Taxes (31%)	Net to Estate	Percent Left to Heirs
1993	61	1,603,347	46,386	856,329	231,576	469,056	29%
1998	66	2,301,039	130,527	1,193,782	343,250	633,480	28%

Assumed Growth Rate: 8% (on Pension balance)

Assumed Estate Tax Rate: 55.00%

Assumed Income Tax Rate on Balance: 31%

marital deduction, or a charitable deduction (see Table III for example of the estate excise tax).

The 15 percent estate excise tax by itself is not that big of a deal. In fact, most people would be happy with a 15 percent estate tax in today's tax environment. However, when you combine the excise tax, estate tax, income tax, state inheritance, and state income taxes there is not much left for the heirs. If, in addition to these taxes, the pension is distributed to grandchildren, and is therefore subject to generation skipping taxes, then it is possible that your heirs may receive an after tax total of *4.3 cents* on each of your hard earned pension dollars. The balance, 95.7 percent may end up in the IRS coffers in the form of the above mentioned taxes. (See also Table IV, "Capital Punishment by Confiscation.")

In conclusion, for individuals who have been successful at developing qualified retirement plan assets, the new "success" tax law necessitates an analysis of the excise income tax (15%) as well as the estate excise tax (15%). With income tax rates at the present level and no guarantee against higher tax rates in the future, a higher distribution at today's tax rates may be a more tax efficient plan for passing these assets to one's loved ones. A combination of maximum distributions and a gifting program to a Supertrust (see Chapter 15) may be the most economical way of protecting your pension from being confiscated at your death by the IRS. In some situations a combination of a lump sum distribution (using 5-or 10-year averaging) from one pension plan and annual distributions may be a prudent course of action.

Table IV

Capital Punishment by Confiscation
Mr. and Mrs. Jonah Michael

Beginning balance in Qualified Plans:	$ 3,000,000
Less Federal Estate Tax (regular):	<1,509,370>
(55% × 2,744,309)	
Balance after Federal Estate Tax	$ 1,490,630
Less: Excess Accumulation Tax	
Amount Accumulated in Plans	$ 3,000,000
Less: Present Value of $150,000	
Annuity (Exemption):	<1,295,400>
Excess subject to Success Tax:	$ 1,704,600
15% Excise Tax	× 15%
	(255,690)
Less: Income Tax Payable by the	
Beneficiary on $1,490,630 @ 39.6%	(590,289)
Amount to Children	$ 644,651
(does not include state or local taxes)	

78.5% to IRS
21.5% to Children
The IRS is the beneficiary of 78.5% of the value of the Pension.
The children receive the remaining 21.5% of the pension assets.

A thorough analysis of all the tax variables is the first step in developing a "tax controlled" distribution plan for IRA and pension assets. For individuals in the retirement plan development stage, now may be the time to review the efficiency of qualified retirement plans for achieving your overall financial goals. Perhaps a cutback or even termination of the qualified plan should be considered. Certainly, it is time to examine alternative non-qualified retirement planning techniques.

Table V

Present Value of an Annuity for Life Expectancy
(Exempt Amount of Pensions at Death)
Note: The exemption amount decreases with age.

Age in 1993	Annual Annuity of $144,551*	Annual Annuity of $150,000**
50	$1,254,963	$1,302,270
51	1,243,673	1,290,555
52	1,231,864	1,278,300
53	1,219,505	1,265,475
54	1,206,654	1,252,140
55	1,193,269	1,238,250
56	1,179,334	1,223,790
57	1,164,806	1,208,715
58	1,149,701	1,193,040
59	1,133,988	1,176,753
60	1,117,755	1,159,890
61	1,101,031	1,142,535
62	1,083,843	1,124,700
63	1,066,208	1,106,400
64	1,048,096	1,087,605
65	1,029,391	1,068,195
66	1,010,065	1,048,140
67	990,059	1,027,380
68	969,402	1,005,945
69	948,182	983,925
70	926,471	961,395
71	904,369	938,460
72	881,891	915,135
73	858,994	891,375
74	835,577	867,075
75	811,567	842,160
76	786,892	816,555
77	761,625	790,335
78	735,851	763,590
79	709,789	736,545
80	683,654	709,425

* Calculated by multiplying $144,551 (1993 indexed amount) times the IRS Table R 10% Annuity Factor at various ages. Regs. Sec. 20.2031-7. The actual percentage may change each month. Use this column if "Grandfather Election" was made.
** Calculated by multiplying $150,000 times the IRS Table R 10% Annuity Factor for various ages. Assumes "Grandfather Election" was not made on 1988 income tax return.

22

How Are the Survivorship Life Insurance Plans Jointly Insuring Two People Being Used in Estate Solutions Today?

by Raymond F. Ciccarelli

Raymond Ciccarelli is co-owner and Vice-President of Ciccarelli Advisory Services, Inc. with offices in Rochester, New York; Naples and Ft. Myers, Florida. Mr. Ciccarelli has been licensed in the securities business when he was 18 and since, has developed a large financial consulting practice in the New York area. His firm has been an innovator of the Living Trust concept for the past 10 years. He brings a practical background to the process and implementation of Living Trusts as well as other creative estate planning techniques. Mr. Ciccarelli holds his Series 7 license with a registered broker/dealer and his insurance license.

Nothing in life stays simple once you bring the U. S. tax code into the picture. Because life insurance enjoys various income tax advantages, sophisticated tax minds devise products that have more to do with clever tax strategies than stranded widows. Life insurance often shields the affluent against the peril of a forced sale of assets at bargain prices to pay estate taxes which are due in cash nine months after death. As a tax shelter, life insurance has at present no rival. Not only does the inside buildup of cash value escape current taxation, the death benefits are tax-free to the beneficiaries.

Though survivorship ("second-to-die") life insurance came into being following the 1981 tax reform, only recently has its cleverness leaked beyond the cable of tax lawyers, CPAs, and "advanced underwriters." The product benefits the very rich more than anyone else, but it has enough intriguing wrinkles to be of interest to the merely affluent.

In 1981, Congress established the unlimited marital deduction, which allows a spouse to bequeath any or all of his or her estate to the surviving partner without the surviving spouse incurring any federal estate taxes. This allows the surviving spouse to defer federal estate taxes until his or her death. However, this act did not eliminate federal estate taxes due upon the survivor's death. If the surviving spouse had an estate larger than the $600,000 exempted from federal estate taxes under the uniform tax credit, the heirs still needed a way to pay the estate tax, which rather quickly jumps to 55 percent. (State death taxes often kick in before $600,000 as well.)

Enter the "second-to-die" policy, which pays only one death benefit upon the death of the surviving spouse. Since, according to actuarial odds, the insurer will have the use of premium monies for a longer time (waiting for two people to die instead of one), the internal cost of insurance (known as the mortality charge) will be significantly lower than in an individual life policy. For example, if the usual probability of death is one out of one thousand, we add another life with a probability of one out of one thousand in a survivorship policy. The multiple effect means that the joint probability of death is one out of ten thousand. That really reduces mortality costs. On a survivorship life policy insuring a 63 year old couple, the first year internal cost of insurance is about $100–$200 for a one million dollar death benefit, which is less than the mortality charge in a single life policy on a 15 year old child. (These costs will vary from company to company.)

What is the big deal? The monies you allocate to a modern competitive permanent contract today are used to pay for internal policy charges with whatever is left after these charges land in interest earning cash value accounts. The largest internal cost in a policy is the mortality charge or the cost of insurance. The other charges, generally $100–$400 for administrative expenses are relatively insignificant in a large policy. Therefore, if you can lower the mortality charge within a policy significantly by adding another life, you earn more interest for your dollars; the true cost of the death benefit is reduced and the accumulation of cash within the policy is increased geometrically. Each year, as you grow older the mortality charge increases, however by overfunding the contract in the early years, you may reduce or control this cost in future years. While not within the scope of this article, *"overfunding"* is a crucial concept for you to understand before purchasing a policy. *Bargain hunting: beware of bargains in parachutes, life preservers, fire extinguishers, brain operations, and "second to die" survivorship life policies!*

What does all this have to do with *maximizing gifts* and *estate taxes?* Who is affected by the most confiscatory tax in the U.S. Tax Code (federal estate taxes)? Anyone who has an estate of $600,000 or larger (or expects through appreciation of assets to surpass the $600,000 threshold) has a federal estate tax liability of 37–60 percent looming over his or her estate like a deep, dark thunder storm. It is relatively simple to shelter up to $1,200,000. What planning is available for estates in excess of $1,200,000? The tax code allows individuals to gift monies during their lifetime to reduce their estate. Developing a gifting program using your annual gift tax exclusions and/or your lifetime unified credit equivalent is the most widely used technique today to reduce the estate tax liability on your estate.

For example, Bill and Marge have an estate of $5,500,000 and have three children. Their present federal estate tax liability is over $2,000,000 and they are reinvesting much of their income. (More assets ultimately mean more estate taxes) They realize that for each $10,000 of appreciation within their estate "Uncle Sam" (their unwritten and unwanted beneficiary) would receive $5,500+ (55%) in taxes upon the death of the *surviving* spouse. However, by making use of their gift tax annual exclusions they have developed a gifting program. They gift $20,000 per year to each of their three children for a total of $60,000 a year. They have helped their children to develop investment programs with these gifts in an effort to prepare them for the responsibility of handling assets. Each time they gift $60,000 they are saving $33,000 in federal estate taxes.

By simple mathematics Bill and Marge came to the conclusion that their gifts of $60,000 (less than 1.5 percent of the estate) would hardly put a dent in their estate tax liability, even over an extended period of time. They decided to make use of $300,000 of Bill's Unified Credit by making a gift of $300,000 to a trust (5.4 percent of their present estate) for the benefit of their three children. Bill and Marge asked how they could maximize the effectiveness of their gifting program. Their planner explained to them that all future appreciation on this $300,000 gift would be exempt from Federal Estate taxes on their estate. In order to maximize the gift they could allocate that gift to a Supertrust funded with life insurance on their lives.

Here is where the magic comes in. Imagine a savings vehicle that earns 7 percent + income tax free on a $300,000 gift and has an immediate *estate* and *income tax free* appreciation of $2,000,000+ upon death, guaranteed whether Bill and Marge live for five or twenty-five more years. This is the magic of *survivorship life*. They have *maximized* the effectiveness of their $300,000 gift. By the magic of compound interest, $300,000 may well be worth $3,000,000–$4,000,000 by the time a death benefit is paid out *income* and *estate tax-free*. The net result is by *maximizing* the use of gifts they will have effectively transferred the bulk of their estate to their children instead of the IRS. They have effectively compounded the value of a $300,000 gift by more than six times.

The moral of the survivorship story might be that the wealthy are different: they have better tax advisors. But in this great country there are an appreciable number of people who by many standards aren't wealthy, but who need to think about estate protection because their houses have appreciated to the half-million or even million dollar mark or a business they struggled to build for a lifetime has appreciated significantly. I must stress that it is a necessity to have a competent team of advisors work out the technical details of an estate plan tailored to your individual situation. A properly drafted trust document, as well as a properly funded Survivorship policy, can go a long way in keeping your assets in the family.

23

How Much Can We Learn from Attending Seminars and Conferences?

by Deborah A. Clementi

Debi Clementi's past experience includes working with a number of businesses and organizations including: International College of Naples, Advisory Board Member; Special Olympics, Philharmonic Center for the Arts, Presidents Council; Girls, Inc., Honorary Board Member; Fine Arts Society, Founder. She developed "Concerts in the Park," Special Olympics Day and Christmas in the City, in cooperation with the City of Naples Department of Parks and Recreation in Naples, Florida. Debi has developed a series of seminar techniques and public presentations on organizational development and public relations techniques for individuals and businesses both in the arts and in the financial services area. She has worked with the Miami City Ballet, and the Philharmonic Center for the Arts in Collier County on the coordination and rehearsals with more than 70 children participating

in the annual "Nutcracker" performance. Debi was nominated for "Woman of the Year" in Collier County in 1981. She is currently involved in the travel industry and resides in Naples with her husband Louis and children, Tiffany and Louie.

We are always learning. To grow older is not to stop the maturing process, regardless of the area of concentration. Knowing your financial status and keeping current on issues that may effect you is a never-ending process.

Conferences, workshops, and seminars can help. They provide a setting to bring up questions for which you need to find answers. Rampant changes in tax laws and economics can be boiled down to non-threatening, more easily understood material. What appears to be a simple novice question can end up being more difficult to answer.

What is your financial status? Few people really know what their net worth, true cash flow, or tax liabilities are. Where do you want to be five years from now? What does financial independence mean to you? Are in a position to continue your desired lifestyle? Will you outlive your legacy?

Take initial steps. Learn the questions you should be asking. Learn about areas that are specific to your own planning. Stimulate your thinking and solutions will arise.

Attending financial conferences meets at least three important objectives:

First, you can familiarize yourself with the professional(s) presenting and work towards finding the proper individuals to work with. The individuals you choose to work with can be the key to positioning yourself in a successful financial matter.

Second, you have an incredible opportunity to gain financial knowledge and begin the process of comparing and qualifying the financial and estate planning guidance you receive.

Third, you will have an opportunity to ask questions in a noncommittal, non-threatening environment.

Not all sessions are worth attending, but I have seen the results from people who are motivated to act because of the initial material presented in a conference setting. This motivation resulted in solutions to many problems, even some problems that they may have been unaware of.

There are some basic buzzwords and questions you should familiarize yourself with, many of which have already been discussed in Parts I and II of this book:

Living Trust	Estate Planner
Living Will	Investment Adviser
Life Insurance-Fixed	Mutual Funds
(universal, interest-sensitive,	Retirement Benefits
term, participating)	Unit Trusts
Variable Life Insurance	Calculating Cost Basis
Variable Annuities	Health Care Surrogate
Joint Survivor Life	Durable Power of Attorney
Stocks	Executor Duties
Bonds	Guardianship
Charitable Trusts	Net Worth
Financial Planner	Gross Tax Payable

If you attend financial conferences with an open mind, they will provide you with a vast array of information. They can help lead you and your family to a successful financial future. Remember, though, this is not a "do-it-yourself" solution. Find the right team to work with and start by providing information about you and your family. From here questions will gear you to the appropriate planning areas to concentrate on.

A proper place to start is by recording the know facts about your status, and then openly discussing your objectives and concerns.

Here's an outline of some of the things you should know about yourself before attending conferences:

Personal data on you and your spouse
Children's family data
Your health
State of Residence

Total property owned including how it is held
(jointly or individually):

Household property	Notes receivable
Personal property	Business interest
Residence	Other property

Other real estate	Loans payable
Bank accounts	Mortgages outstanding
Insurance plans	Marketable securities
Annuities	

Facts about your will, trust
Facts about your business, is there a continuation plan?
Health insurance plans/nursing home insurance

Sources of income:
Investment
Social security
Earned income
Retirement/pension amounts, and spousal benefits
Health care plan
Disability plan

What were your income tax liabilities in past years?
Anticipated future income tax liabilities
Special bequests
Charitable intentions
Factors that will change your desired cash flow
Who will inherit your legacy and how?
Are you comfortable with your planning that is in place now?
Who makes financial decisions? Will this change?
Are you currently gifting to children?
Is your estate subject to taxes?
How did you file for the grandfathering provisions relative to
        excise taxes (income and estate) due on pension benefits?
Any trusts for you or a beneficiary?
Expected inheritances and will this effect your estate plan?

These questions are just the beginning. Seek professional guidance to learn more about the very important details that will make a difference to your planning success or failure. Take advantage of the knowledge that can be shared at financial conferences.

24

How Do We Begin to Analyze the Insurance Industry with Respect to a Particular Company and Product Type?

by Louis A. Clementi

Louis Clementi received his Bachelor of Science degree in business administration at the State University of New York College at Buffalo. He is president and owner of Estate Planners, Inc., a Florida Corporation which provides services to financial professionals, including family members. His expertise is in administrative systems and health and financial underwriting for life insurance purposes. One of the founders of the Naples planning offices, his company is responsible for the design, implementation, and operation of the computer systems, administration of the Naples offices, in addition to coordination and communications with suppliers and outside consultants. Lou and his

wife, Debi, were two of the founders of The Naples Fine Arts Society and have been active supporters of many charities in the Naples area, including Special Olympics, The Philharmonic, (TECH) Training and Educational Center for the Handicapped, and Mental Health Association.

Start first by choosing a competent, independent professional, well-versed in the complicated arena of insurance companies and products. You do not want to take the intensive time to become a specialist in insurance specifics that do not apply to your own individual needs. You do, however, want to be familiar with insurance trends, what makes a company solvent, enabling it to produce the expected results, and know that you are receiving a modern day competitive program in which to participate. Do your homework so you may feel comfortable that performance can mirror current and ongoing economies of scale.

Insurance companies are unique in that they now provide investment management as well as pay death claims, which can be significantly higher than premiums paid. The results are statistically calculated actuarially by the health and age of the insured.

Looking to the financial solvency of a company, several rating agencies have entered the reporting arena:

A. M. Best Company

A. M. Best Company located in Oldwick, New Jersey, annually pre-pares comprehensive statistical reports on the financial position, history, and operating results of most life insurance companies. These reports, which are included in the annual *Best's Insurance Reports* were first published in 1906 and are considered to be the analytical benchmark for the industry.

The objective of Best's rating system is to evaluate the various factors effecting the overall performance of an insurance company in order to provide an opinion as to the company's overall relative financial strength and ability to meet contractual obligations. Their reports are based on actual visits to the life insurance company. The ratings are defined as follows:

A++, A+	Superior. Very strong ability to meet obligations
A, A-	Excellent. Strong ability to meet obligations
B++, B+	Very Good. Strong ability to meet obligations
B, B-	Good. Adequate ability to meet obligations
C++, C+	Fair. Reasonable ability to meet obligations
C, C-	Marginal. Currently has the ability to meet obligations
D	Below minimum standards
E	Under state supervision
F	In liquidation

Duff & Phelps

Duff & Phelps, Inc. located in Chicago, Illinois prepares an in-depth analysis of both domestic and international insurance companies. The rating process used is a combination of quantitative and qualitative analysis.

According to Duff & Phelps, a number of quantitative factors are considered in assigning ratings. The more important factors measure profitability, operating leverage, and surplus adequacy. Major shifts in interest rates are a key consideration, and whether a company is more or less sensitive to underwriting and business cycles is also important.

Major qualitative factors include: parent, affiliate or subsidiary, and general management's capability.

The ratings are subscribed for and paid by the company and can be assigned as follows:

AAA	Highest claims-paying ability. Negligible risk.
AA+, AA, AA-	Very high claims-paying ability. Modest risk.
A+, A, A-	High claims-paying ability. Variable risk over time.
BBB+, BBB, BBB-	Below average claims-paying ability. Considerable variability in risk over time.
BB+, BB, BB-	Uncertain claims-paying ability. Protective factors are subject to change with adverse economy.
CCC	Substantial risk regarding claims-paying ability. Likely to be placed under state insurance department supervision.

Moody's Investor Service

Moody's Investor Service located in New York City is a leading credit rating agency that has been evaluating life insurance companies since the 1970s. Currently, Moody's has rating relationships with over 200 insurance groups and financial strength ratios on over 70 insurance companies.

The rating process is both dynamic and intensive. Analysts meet with insurance companies to analyze the structure and prospects for the company. Several factors that are considered include quality of assets, product mix, management of the company (both style and strategy), and capital adequacy. Moody's insurance financial strength ratings assess the ability of insurance companies to repay punctually senior policyholder obligations and claims. According to Moody's, insurance companies "rated" Aaa offer exceptional financial security. While the financial strength of companies is likely to change, such changes as can be visualized are most unlikely to impair their fundamentally strong position. Their rating system is as follows:

Aaa	Exceptional security. Unlikely to be affected by change.
Aa	Excellent security. Lower than Aaa because long-term risks appear somewhat larger.
A	Good security. Possibly susceptible to future impairment.
Baa	Adequate security. Possibly susceptible to future impairment.
Ba	Questionable security. Ability to meet obligations may be moderate.
B	Poor security. Assurance of punctual payment of obligations is small over the long run.
Caa	Very poor security. There may be elements of danger regarding the payment of obligations.
Ca	Extremely poor security. Companies are often in default.
C	Lowest security. Extremely poor prospects of offering financial security.

Understanding the ratings of a company is a very preliminary step to doing your homework. Your team of advisers should understand the direction and nature of the company in their design of their products and origin of their profits. A company must be in a position to meet its contractual obligations. Take a look at its investment portfolio, what types of assets are included, what quality are they, and what is the net return the company is realizing? With the interest rate trends and conservative investment methods of insurance companies, we are not seeing the disparity in performance results in recent years that used to be a critical factor in picking the company and products one should choose to use. Most companies invest in bonds and mortgages positioned mostly in high quality, and very little is allocated to stocks.

The company's surplus is very important and yearly profits can help add to this surplus. Surplus and investment reserves are what we call a contingency fund for difficult times. An insurer's level of security can be measured in part by the ratio of its surplus capital to total assets owned. It also provides a measuring stick for how well the company is keeping pace with business growth. Their own capital over reserves that are set aside to meet future obligations to policyholders and their beneficiaries, should be a positive number. In most cases, professionals in the business will look at a net capital position of 10.0 percent or greater to provide a good comfort level to meet the need to pay benefits on a timely basis. An insurer's investment of assets must fit the rates and timing of future claims and payments. Additionally, a steady flow of income is fundamental to an insurer's strength. Income results from premiums and investments. A competitive edge should be achieved by offering the right products, backed by sound investment management and proper and efficient servicing systems. Insurance companies generally have a core business, and should be in the area you are looking for. For example, the estate planning arena is a specialized area tailored generally to older ages and larger death benefits and premium amounts than the average industry offers. Companies have to do an incredible job of managing mortality risks and investment performance. For a long time actual experience proved to be better than "illustrated" performance. This is not true in the 1990s. Illustrations are grossly misused and should only provide you with an "illustration" of what makes the plan tick and how it works. The illustrations should use percentages that are conservative and in focus with today's rates. Also, the contract is reviewed to see what the contractual guarantees are.

Companies will credit your cash values by using either a "portfolio rate" or a "new money rate." There is a difference given certain economic factors and trends. Cash value performance adds or subtracts from expected results on your policy:

Portfolio Rates: The product is supported with the entire block of investments purchased over time for the line of business. Assets are not allocated to particular products. This allows for a more predictable pattern of investment yields, cash value rates to the policyholder generally will not change when there are only small fluctuations in the portfolio rate. This can be a good system when rates fall, and tends to be less competitive when rates rise.

The New Money Rate System: Interest rates credited to cash values are based on current yields using recently invested assets. This can lead to a more volatile pattern of investment yields. Large fluctuations in interest rates are credited to the product as they occur. This is good system when rates rise, but tends to be less competitive when rates fall.

It is important for a client to work with a consultant who works with the specialized types of product he or she needs. The industry is so widespread, and the products so vastly different, that only someone experienced in reviewing companies and knowing their products can assist you in obtaining a favorable contract that will continue your estate plan and benefit you and your beneficiaries.

25

What Is Wrong with Using an Ordinary Will as My Key Estate Planning Document?

by LaDonna J. Cody

LaDonna J. Cody is a tax attorney in Fort Myers, Florida, practicing in the areas of real estate, estate and probate law. She is a graduate of Florida International University with a Bachelor of Arts degree in international relations, received her Juris Doctor from Nova Law Center in Ft. Lauderdale, and attended the University of Miami Master of Law of Taxation program. Ms. Cody is a widely acclaimed speaker throughout Southern Florida on the subject of estate planning, estate taxation and trusts, and has appeared on the "Financial Planning Forum" television show in Tampa as the guest host. She is a member of the Lee County Bar Association, the Florida Bar Association, and the American Bar Association in the International Law, Real

Estate and Probate, and Taxation sections. A founding and senior partner of a large law firm with offices in several cities throughout Florida, Ms. Cody is currently a sole practitioner.

When an individual is planning the distribution of his or her estate, all assets the person owns or has control over must be considered. Also, assets owned in any form of joint ownership must also be taken into consideration. Assets passing through the will are the assets which are subject to probate. Probate is the orderly distribution of a person's assets after his or her death, monitored by the judicial system. Not all assets a person owns will necessarily be subject to the probate system. In general, life insurance, annuities, pension plans, IRAs, and jointly owned assets are not part of the probate estate because either a beneficiary has previously been named on the title of the asset, or the asset passes by operation of law to the joint owner. Keeping this in mind, using an ordinary will may not always achieve all an individual's objectives in disposing of his or her assets after death. For instance, let's say a husband and wife have their attorney draw up their wills giving all their assets to the other spouse in the event of death of one spouse. In the event they die in a common accident, or if one spouse predeceases the surviving spouse, the surviving spouse passes his or her assets to their children in equal shares. This appears to be a fair distribution; however, if a joint asset has been opened with one child as a joint owner or a life insurance policy names another child as the primary beneficiary, then those assets will pass outside of the probate system. A possible uninterested inequitable distribution of assets may occur. It would be wiser to take all assets into account when providing for the orderly distribution of the estate.

A properly drafted will should provide some relief. It can lay out an orderly plan that systematically controls the distribution of the estate. A will can eliminate quarrels by family members as to who should receive certain personal property such as a ring or a watch. A person can prename who will be the guardian of the person and property of a minor child. A will can also implement trusts for various beneficiaries. If properly drafted, a will could create the coordination of non-probate assets, i.e., integration with a revocable living trust.

The will is not necessarily the panacea of estate planning. If an asset is being disposed of through the will, this means it must be probated. Probate can bring with it delays in the estate assets being available for the family or other beneficiary's use. An effective estate plan should provide a transfer of assets with minimal delay. Also, the expenses and costs involved in probate can be more costly than looking at probate alternatives.

Probate alternatives are ways of passing assets to loved ones and other beneficiaries, but, because of the way they are structured or titled, the assets pass to the intended beneficiary without being bogged down by probate.

A number of examples of probate alternatives exist. One would be life insurance and other life insurance products such as annuities. Life insurance allows a person to name a beneficiary. Generally, upon the beneficiary providing a death certificate of the deceased person, the benefits of the life insurance flow directly to the recipient by contract, thus avoiding probate. "The Estate" should not be named as the beneficiary unless it is specifically intended that the proceeds of the life insurance be probated.

This would also be true of pension plans. IRAs on the other hand should probably have the spouse, if there is a surviving spouse, as the named beneficiary to take advantage of the spousal rollover. A Spousal Rollover is where a surviving spouse may "roll over" the assets in the deceased spouses's IRA to the IRA of the surviving spouse, thus avoiding immediate income tax consequences of the assets in the IRA.

Holding assets in joint tenancy is another probate alternative. If a husband and wife own assets jointly and one of them passes away, the survivor receives the assets immediately without having to go through the probate system. However, when the survivor passes away, or if both of them pass away in a common accident, then the assets would have to be probated. Often, unmarried persons (mother/child) place assets in joint name without even considering the consequence. If both persons did not contribute to the joint account, a gift has been created by placing the non-contributing person's name on the account. Depending on the amount of the gift, a gift tax return may have to be filed with the Internal Revenue Service. Also, unintended estate and income tax consequences may occur. The consequences of joint tenancy must be carefully reviewed before using it as a method of estate planning.

By using a living trust, the probate system can be avoided. A living trust (also known as a Grantor Trust or Revocable Trust) is a contract between the Grantor (the person who sets up the trust) with the Trustee (the person or institution who will administer the trust) for the benefit of the beneficiary. Often the grantor, trust, and beneficiary are one in the same person. The assets of the living trust can usually be distributed more quickly and more privately than the probate estate. With rare exceptions, avoiding the court system reduces the costs and expenses of the estate. However, an aspect of probate is the extinguishment of claims of creditors to the estate after a very short claims period. An evaluation of the capability of the trustee to manage the distribution should be predetermined and perhaps co-trustees may be named. (An example would be a family member along with a Trust Company.) In the living trust settlement, your successor trustee(s) will not have the supervision of the circuit court in the handling of the estate, such supervision does occur in a probate estate. It is important that you have faith and confidence in the honesty, integrity, and ability of the successor trustee(s) you appoint to wind up your affairs without court supervision. Many people choose a son or daughter as successor trustee. However, sibling rivalry often does not arise until both spouses have passed away, and often the relatives (son, daughter, brother, sister, etc.) will not have the experience, continuity, or ability of a commercial trust company.

Given the foregoing, what is the best choice for distributing your estate? The vast majority of retirees, who are exposed to the living trust, choose to go with the living trust. Property equalization of assets between spouses, along with completing much of the work up front, can lead to savings in time and expenses, which is a major factor in this decision.

26

How Do We Decide
and Prepare for
Custodian and Guardianship
Appointments?

by Joe B. Cox

Joe B. Cox is a partner with a major law firm with offices in: Naples and West Palm, Florida; and Stanford, Grenwich, and Hartford, Connecticut. He has been a practicing attorney for over 20 years in the areas of taxation and estate planning. A graduate of Oklahoma State University, he received his Juris Doctor (J.D.) from the University of Tulsa, and his Masters of Law in Estate Planning (LL.M.) from the University of Miami. Mr. Cox is one of 13 attorneys in Florida (and the only attorney in Southwest Florida) who is certified in both Taxation and Estate Planning and Probate Law. He is a member of the Oklahoma and Florida Bar Associations' sections on Taxation and Real Property, and Probate and Trust Law. Mr. Cox is a widely acclaimed

speaker throughout the State of Florida because of his knowledge and experience in the area of advanced estate planning techniques and his ability to communicate with audiences. Mr. Cox has published extensively on various topics involving estate planning.

Since we are all living longer and health care professionals have greatly improved techniques of maintaining our lives, it is quite possible a time may come when many of us will not be able to manage our own affairs. Without adequate preplanning, the need for guardianship may well become apparent.

My answer will explain what a Florida guardianship is and how planning can avoid it. You should check with your state of residence to determine whether the following information applies.

There are numerous "terms of art" inherent to an understanding of Florida guardianships. There are different types of guardians. One is a "limited guardian" appointed by a court to exercise some of the tasks necessary to care for the ward's person and property. A "plenary guardian" is one appointed to exercise all legal rights and powers of the ward.

The incapacitated person ("ward") is an individual who has been judicially determined to lack the capacity to manage some or all of his or her property and may be unable to manage his or her health care needs.

An individual has the right in Florida to name a "pre-need guardian" by written declaration to serve in the event of the incapacity of the declarant.

Florida also recognizes the "natural guardian", who is the natural mother and/or father of a minor child (under age 18).

Any time a guardianship is required, the family should be prepared to encounter guardian and attorney's fees.

In addition, there will be court costs and professional fees for psychiatrists, psychologists, gerontologists, and other experts who might be required to testify. The expenses can be substantial. Further, many of these expenses are repeated each year the guardianship is in effect.

In order for an adjudication of incapacity to occur, a court hearing takes place in which the professionals mentioned above will be involved, and many could testify. All hearings relating to guardianships are transcribed in the event an appeal is desired by any interested party.

A guardianship must be brought in the circuit court for the Florida county in which the potential ward resides. A procedure also exists for appointment of an emergency temporary guardian if the court finds there is imminent danger to health of the potential ward or that his or her property is in danger of being wasted or lost. One of the planning tools we utilize today, where the possibility of future guardianship is even remote, is a written declaration appointing a pre-need guardian. This allows a personal decision as to who will serve as guardian if the need ever arises. A resident of Florida who is over age 18 is qualified to act as a Florida guardian. A non-resident may serve as guardian if related to the potential ward by blood or marriage. The courts are extremely careful not to appoint a guardian where a conflict of interest might be present or potentially present.

Financial institutions are sometimes appointed guardians of property, but seldom appointed guardians of the person. Before an individual may be appointed a Florida guardian, he or she must complete an application for appointment to be reviewed by the court. This lists the applicant's qualifications to serve as a guardian. Most corporate guardians are exempt from this disclosure procedure. A Florida guardian, after appointment, must receive a minimum of eight hours of training through a court approved organization. A Florida guardianship begins with the filing of a detailed petition to determine capacity. This is a highly detailed court document and involves a significant amount of time for proper preparation. Formal notice is then given to the named subject of the guardianship, and the court appoints an attorney to represent the potential ward's interest.

An examining committee of three persons is appointed when the petition to determine capacity is filed. One member must be a psychiatrist or a physician; another may be a psychologist, gerontologist, or registered nurse; and the third member may be an unrelated lay person. The committee must examine the guardianship subject and must file a written report within 15 days after appointment. The report is required to include diagnosis, prognosis, recommended course of treatment, evaluation of the subject's ability to retain rights, a description of matters with respect to which the person lacks capacity of exercise rights, and an assessment of information provided by the subject's family physician.

After the committee's report is filed, a hearing is held in which the court renders an adjudication. If the court determines the subject to be incapacitated, an order is rendered determining incapacity and its extent.

The rights that may be removed from an adjudicated ward include the rights to marry, vote, hold a driver's license, change residence, be employed, contract, sue, manage property, make gifts, consent to medical treatment, or make decisions affecting his or her social environment. The determination as to incapacity can be extremely broad as to what rights may be removed from the ward. An alternative approach, known as a "voluntary guardianship," is available and permits an adjudication of mental competency coupled with an adjudication of incapacity of caring for property by reason of age or physical infirmity. The petition in such a proceeding must be by the subject and must be accompanied by a physician's certification that the subject is competent to understand the nature of the guardianship and the resulting delegation of authority.

An order appointing a Florida guardian will state whether the guardianship is plenary or limited, and will detail the rights removed from the ward. A guardian's bond will be required, adding to the costs of the proceeding.

The court document issued to a Florida guardian authorizing the guardian to act in a limited or plenary manner is the guardian's "Letters of Guardianship."

Once the Letters are issued, the guardian may exercise only those rights delegated.

The guardian must file an annual report showing implementation of the guardianship plan and is required to include the following: provisions for medical and personal care, social services, residential setting meeting the ward's needs, and any periodic examinations necessary for further evaluation. The plan is based upon the recommendation of the examining committee.

An annual guardianship plan must be filed stating where the ward is and has been maintained, whether the current residential setting is best suited for the ward, and a plan for the coming year proposing a residential setting best meeting the ward's needs.

A Florida guardian of the property must also file an annual accounting, detailing the year's receipts and disbursements on behalf of the ward.

Many acts taken for granted in an individual's management of his or her affairs must be supported by court order in a guardianship situation. This adds to the costs of guardianship. A Florida guardianship may be terminated by the ward's proving capacity. This determination will be made only after a hearing is held with prior notice to all interested parties. If a restoration of capacity is found, the guardian files a final accounting for court review, returns all property to the ward, and the guardianship is terminated.

How, then, can a guardianship and its complexity be avoided?

1. Create a Revocable Living Trust that is funded for alternative management of your assets when you are unable to manage them;

2. Create a Durable Power of Attorney with someone in whom you have confidence for assistance in managing assets which are not in the Trust, or assistance in transferring assets to the Trust. (The holder of the Power of Attorney can also perform various ministerial acts that the Trustee might not perform.);

3. Create a Durable Power of Attorney for health care;

4. Appoint a health care surrogate; and

5. Make a Living Will.

Prepared as a complementary system by competent counsel, these documents, interacting together, result in the availability of trusted surrogates to carry on an individual's affairs despite incapacity, eliminating the need for a Florida guardianship.

27

How Can We Defer Taxes Using Tax-Deferred Annuities?

by Anthony J. Curatolo

Anthony Curatolo is President of A. J. Curatolo Financial Service Inc., a Registered Investment Advisory Firm specializing in financial planning and tax preparation. Mr. Curatolo is a member of the NASD in the State of New York and Florida. He holds life, annuity, and disability insurance licenses. Curatolo holds frequent seminars dealing with money management. His civic activities include board member for the YMCA and the International Association of Financial Planners chaptered in Western New York.

Inching through the jungle of accounting and tax laws is very treacherous. Now is the time to read the map on tax planning, for the consequences of not doing so are very costly.

One of the most popular consumer-driven investment vehicles of the '80s, continuing into the '90s is the Tax-Deferred Annuity Program. Tax-deferred annuities are saving programs offered through life insurance companies. They are distributed through banks, brokerage firms, insurance agencies, and independent financial professionals. Today, tax-deferred annuities are capturing a large part of the market as an alternative to bank CDs. Annuities are rapidly capturing millions of investment dollars moreover than the mutual fund industry.

A client will typically choose an annuity for two reasons, as a hedge against other positions in his or her portfolio, and a desire to achieve tax favored growth with ease of management and relative liquidity. Fixed annuities are considered *safe, secure*. They are backed by insurance company assets, and guarantee your principal will remain intact.

A modern, up-to-date plan will not deduct a sales charge from your investment. Instead, the insurance company, like a bank with their CDs, determines a minimum holding period and can assess a penalty for early withdrawal. A report is sent each calendar year to the policy holder or "owner," but no 1099s need be given to your accountant. Asset accumulating in an annuity require no reporting for state or federal income taxes.

If a withdrawal is taken prior to age 59½, there may be a 10 percent government penalty, unless waived due to death, disability, or a systematic payment based over your lifetime.

A tax deferred annuity, whether fixed, or variable requires three designated parties:

#1 ANNUITANT   An annuitant is the person whose age calculates and sets a time period for when and how income will be payable during the life if annuitized (optional) or at death; the proceeds are generally payable in a single sum.

#2 OWNER   The owner can be the same as the annuitant or different. The owner is taxed on distributions. Some contracts allow for a joint or contingent owner.

#3 BENEFICIARY   The beneficiary is the person who receive the benefits of the contract proceeds when the owner or annuitant dies.

Case Study #1

Situation: John, wife Sue, 50-year-old executive, two grown children, adjusted gross income over $50,000, banking $1,000 a month after expenses, and has maxed out the amount with a 401k plan at work.

Objective: Save for retirement.

Case Study #2

Situation: Mary, widow, three grown children, and three grandchildren.

Objective: Cash flow is sufficient for now, does not need to increase income above current level of Social Security, pension benefits, and stock dividends.

An Annuity would help John, Sue, and Mary in these ways:

1. Avoid taxes

2. Accumulate for later years

3. Plan estate for children (no probate)

When considering money management today, I have found generally, that clients may prefer to give up aggressive growth tactics for guarantees. As a final note, all annuities do the same thing—save money—but all life insurance companies have different bells and whistles. Before investing in an annuity, research, at minimum, their surrender charge, interest credit period, distribution of income, age limits, and rating (stay with A+ companies by A.M. Best).

Above all, don't choose the highest yield, but rather be more concerned with their track record.

As always, knowing the ground rules makes for a happier return and safe trip through that tax jungle. Refer to Sandra C. Fournie's article, "What Should We Look for when Considering a Tax-Deferred Annuity?" for tips to participating in an annuity plan.

28

The Pitfalls of Estate Planning with "Joint Tenancy" Only

by Joseph Ferraina

Joseph Ferraina is a partner of a Western New York financial and estate consulting firm. A graduate of the State University College at Buffalo, he received his Bachelor of Science degree in consumer business studies and from Erie Community College his Associates degree in business administration. He holds his life and disability insurance license, and an NASD Series 7 License with a registered broker/dealer.

A simple definition of joint tenancy is that two or more people own property together and the survivor will own the property at the death of the joint owner.

The surviving owner is vested automatically to receive the jointly owned property regardless of a will. Joint tenancy supersedes a will designation.

Joint ownership avoids probate completely, which is its main advantage, but most jointly owned property is in the name of a husband and wife in which the property ultimately becomes probatable upon the death of both owners. The surviving spouse could name a joint owner upon the death of their spouse, for example, a grown child, to avoid the probate upon the second death, but this process is usually not recommended for the following reasons:

1. Upon your death, your asset will pass directly to the child you name as joint owner. This may be fine if you have two or more children.
2. The child who is named joint owner is just that—joint owner, he or she has all the same rights as you do, such as liquidating the asset.
3. Your asset could be subject to your child's creditors in the case of a lawsuit or divorce.
4. Joint tenancy eliminates the stepped-up basis of your asset. An example being a house jointly held by you and your child. When you pass away, your child owns one half of the home at your cost basis. He or she only inherits your half without being subjected to taxes when he or she sells. Eventually when the child sells that house, it is the price you paid for the house that is figured for income tax purposes on the child's half. If you leave your child that same home through your will or living trust, when that house is sold, the cost basis is as of your death and not as of the day of purchase, which could be 20 or 30 years previous.
5. Multiple marriages in a lifetime could also be a problem with joint tenancy. You may want your second wife, for example, to live in the house until her death and then your home (or asset) is to pass to your children, not hers. This may not happen if your home is jointly owned.

6. If your child names a power of attorney to handle his or her affairs, at anytime that power of attorney could deplete your assets.

7. It is important to note that one of the first areas the "IRS" looks at in an estate audit is assets jointly owned with a child. If you name your child as a joint owner, and adequate consideration was not exchanged, then a "gift" has been effected as of the date you retitled your deed, property, or the name of an investment account. The amount of the gift would need to be determined, and a gift tax return must be filed in the amount, along with any other gifts, exceeding the allowable annual exclusion for the year.

8. Joint ownership does not reduce estate taxes. Although assets held jointly avoid probate at the joint owner's death, the asset is still subject to estate taxes.

9. Jointly owned property is figured in for health care for the elderly, such as nursing home costs and the ability to receive Medicare or Medicaid. During that crucial time, you should be the one making decisions, not a government agency.

The preceding discusses the major pitfalls of joint tenancy. The major advantages of joint tenancy are that it is simple, inexpensive, and it avoids probate on the first death. The best alternative to joint tenancy I could suggest is to set up a living trust for your estate plan. Allocate and title your assets so that the least negative circumstances apply both during your lifetime and at death.

29

What Ongoing Services Can I Expect from My Advisor?

by Lynn A. Ferraina

Lynn A. Ferraina is a partner of a Western New York financial and estate consulting firm. Lynn's background includes over 18 years in the field of finance, having been an account executive with National Investors Center, a corporate division of Goldome Bank where she was responsible for a $25 million portfolio before starting her own consulting firm in 1985. Lynn is a frequent lecturer on estate and financial techniques, and holds her insurance licenses. She networks with attorneys and accountants for comprehensive solutions on behalf of individuals and businesses.

After many hours of working with a financial professional to design a financial and estate plan particular to your circumstances, the plan is now in effect and complete. *Wrong.* This is just the beginning. The most important factor to choosing your financial advisor is the type of ongoing service he or she provides and commits to. Service is key; we want to make sure our clients' plans continue to meet all their objectives.

So many factors can change from year to year. Some are beyond our control, such as tax law changes by the government, company benefits changes by your place of employment, overall condition of our country's economy, the financial needs of our children and parents, and possible medical devastation to our family assets.

Inflation, recession, stock market, or real estate booms or slumps are all factors that can affect us. In the course of your life, many positive factors can affect you, such as salary increases, promotions and bonuses, a move to a new home or for that matter a new city, a marriage, birth of a child, an inheritance, or a windfall profit perhaps through a sale of a business. Some negative factors that could affect your plan are a loss of a job, a prolonged illness, a death in your family, or if you are self-employed, a decline in business income. These are all reasons why constant monitoring of your plan is so important. This may be done monthly, or every six months, but certainly no less than an annual meeting is an absolute.

A professional will devise a course of action very differently for a 25-year-old, a 45-year-old, or a 65- or 80-year-old, and Investment Planning (asset accumulation), Retirement Planning (living on your asset accumulation), and Estate Planning (preserving your asset accumulation), are all pieces of the services you should be receiving.

At least once a year, your financial professional should schedule a full evaluation of your finances. A balance sheet of all your assets can determine which investments have performed favorably and which have not and the proper adjustments that may need to be planned for. For example, a change in tax laws or your own personal situation might warrant a reallocation of assets from taxable vehicles to tax-free or tax-deferred.

Another part of our responsibility as financial professionals, is to analyze the stability of the companies your investments are placed with. A prime example are assets directed to the banks and insurance companies. As a beginning, a financial professional will have the annual reports for the banks your money is on deposit with and the annual report and A.M. Best recommendation, along with a proper due diligence report for your insurance companies. It is important for an investor to work with strong companies.

Service, service, service is the key to the effectiveness of your financial and estate planning. Because of the importance of the ongoing services your financial professional provides, you should clarify what the ongoing services will be in your first interview. Expect their knowledge to be passed to you by proper implementation of ideas that are created through factual information which must be integrated on your financial journey.

30

What Should We Look for When Considering a Tax-Deferred Annuity?

by Sandra C. Fournie

Sandra Fournie manages and operates Business Programs, Inc., which provides marketing and services to financial professionals including family members. She coordinates the public seminars, processes all advertising and printing, is responsible for media communications and accounting systems for the various independent companies including monthly profit and loss statements and balance sheets. Sandy coordinates systems for client updates and files and audits compliance procedures for the various licenses. She directs and coordinates the continuing education programs offered to legal and financial professionals. Sandy is a certified instructor for the NCFE (National Center for Financial Education) and has been active in Toastmasters International, a volunteer for Special Olympics, and served as a board member of the Junior Achievement Business Leadership Hall of Fame.

There are several factors that should be reviewed and evaluated when considering a tax-deferred annuity. The following annuity checklist should be supportive in assisting your decision to use annuities.

Types of Annuities

Fixed or Variable
- Single Premium Deferred Annuity (SPDA)
- Flexible Premium Deferred Annuity (Flex-pay)
- Immediate Annuity
- Split Annuity (highbred of immediate and SPDA contracts)
- Qualified or Non-tax qualified

Interest rates

- Period of initial guaranteed rate
- Lifetime written guaranteed rate on contract (lowest rate)
- Maturity
- Tiered interest rate—or does all money earn rate?
  How are interest rates declared?
- Renewal history
- Portfolio vs. pod method
- Bail out rate
- Bonus rates (Does contract require annuitization?
  Come on rates?)
- Pricing (How does surrender period, bailout, commission figure in the formula?)

Charges

- Sales, administrative, or expense charges?
  Mortality charges?
- Minimum, maximum deposits
- Surrender Charges

Liquidity

- Partial withdrawals
- Loans
- Bail out
- Guarantee principal-low surrender is calculated
- *Maturity of surrender charges*

Qualifications
- Age limits for issue
- Minimum and maximum investments

Income and Distribution Options
- At what age can distribution be deferred until?
- Partial withdrawals allowed
- Split annuity
- Settlement Options
- Lump sum
- *Maturity of surrender charge*
- Interest only
- Several annuity options including period certain with or without life contingency
- What is annuitizing rate? Are there fees to annuitize?

Choosing a Company
- Statutory profit
- GAAP Profit
- *Capital surplus of company*
- How rated by A.M. Best?
- Historical portfolio earnings
- What does portfolio consist of?
- How much in junk bonds?
- How many mortgages in default?
- Portfolio maturities
- Where is company domiciled?
- Is company registered to do business in Florida?

Miscellaneous
- Assets are probate free as long as there is a named beneficiary other than your "Estate"
- Does company issue annual reports on the account?
- Protection from creditors (For Example: under Florida Homestead Statute protected from Seizure by creditors)

Tax Ramifications
- Tax Deferral
- Owner must be a "person"

- LIFO vs. FIFO (pre-1982 annuities subject to more favorable FIFO rules)
- 1035 exchanges (maintaining FIFO advantage) must be done properly to maintain tax advantage
- No Florida Intangible taxes (for example, exemption from state income taxes)
- Not included to calculate tax on social security benefits
- Not included for AMT taxes
- Not subject to 1099 reporting during accumulation period
- Twelve-month rule on purchase of multiple annuities contracts from same company
- Immediate annuity-exclusion ratio tax break on income from annuitized account
- Ten percent government penalty on withdrawal before age 59½
- How to avoid this penalty?
- Who owns contract? Taxes on death of annuitant, owner, etc., if different people. Spousal rollover, 5 year deferral of income tax option on payout at death of owner or annuitant.
- Transfer of ownership—pre-April 22, 1987 vs. after 4/87
- Can contingent or joint owners be named?

How Can Annuities Be Used?

- Non-qualified (assets reallocated from portfolio of CDs/Real Etate/Securities/Cash)
- Qualified
- IRAs
- TSAs
- SEP IRAs
- Pensions (401(k)s, defined benefit plans)
- Profit Sharing Plans, Keoghs
- Rollovers or 1035 exchanges to continue benefits

For specific information on the above items listed, our readers should contact Ciccarelli Advisory Services, Inc. We can then provide a more comprehensive explanation of the important factors to consider prior to allocating assets to an annuity.

31

How Do I Use a Split Annuity?

by Samuel S. Henderson

Sam Henderson graduated with a Bachelor of Arts degree in economics from the University of Florida in Gainesville. He has since received advanced degrees in financial management and investments from both NCNB National Bank of Florida and Merrill Lynch Pierce Fenner & Smith, where he served as Assistant Vice President and Commercial Lending Officer and Financial Consultant, respectively. He holds his Series 7 NASD license as well as his life and health insurance license from the State of Florida. His 12 years of experience in the financial arena in Southwest Florida has continued with the establishment of Samuel S. Henderson, Independent Financial Consultant, where he specializes in estate and fixed-income solutions.

The split annuity contract has been marketed as the "CD Alternative" or the "Tax Advantaged CD" by the brokerage and life insurance industries. Brokers and agents across the country jumped on the split annuity "bandwagon," and record numbers of those contracts were sold to American investors.

The reason for this popularity? Safety and income. The client could invest an amount of money, usually on a five-year or ten-year basis, have a monthly check, and at the end of the guarantee period have his or her original investment back. Also, a portion of his or her monthly cash flow was tax-free (i.e., on a five year plan, approximately 85 percent of the monthly amount was tax-free).

On the typical split funded contract, the policy owner is purchasing two annuity contracts. Below is an example using a five-year program:

First Contract

A single premium *immediate* annuity is annuitized (paid out to contract holder) over a five-year period on a monthly basis. Payments under an immediate annuity include a portion that is a return of principal to the policyholder. Since a return of principal is excluded from reported income, it is tax-free to the policyholder. Exact calculations are provided by your consultant and should be reviewed thoroughly.

Second Contract

An investment can be made into a single premium *deferred* annuity with a guaranteed interest rate, and be coordinated to the maturity or last month of pay out on the immediate side. The objective is to have the value of the contract at the end of the five years, at minimum, equal your original investment.

Since the earnings are deferred, and continue to build up inside this contract, there are no taxes to be paid. No income is reported on an annuity until it is withdrawn. This second contract may also be structured under a "Variable Annuity Plan." This type of plan allows the same option to defer taxes on earnings until withdrawal; however, the internal investment works differently. Instead of a fixed rate of return, the variable annuity provides the same opportunities and risks of investing in the stock or bond market, very similar to allocating money to mutual funds.

A question that should arise under this form of plan is, what happens when the immediate contract policy expires and there is no more income to be drawn? The deferred annuity quite possibly has accumulated back to or exceeded your original investment. If income is still needed, then perhaps current laws would allow you to adopt a similar "split investment" plan. One program providing income with a growth option in the second plan.

One caveat to be aware of . . . upon a second split, withdrawals from the contract would be subject to 10 percent federal penalty tax if the policyholder is under age $50\frac{1}{2}$. Also, an exclusion from taxes could apply to the second split or income stream, but this would be lower than the initial ratio. If you decide to remove your money from the annuity and allocate these assets to other investments, then federal income taxes are due on the accumulated amount. If a policy owner is less than $59\frac{1}{2}$, a federal penalty could apply. One strategy to consider would be to continue deferring the second contract as is, and utilize a partial withdrawal option annually from the annuity. The contract would incur no penalty and you still have the flexibility to get to your money.

Split funding an annuity contract for the right investor with the right insurance company can be a valuable tool. This concept meets two important needs—income and on a guaranteed contract, accumulation back to the initial deposit. A variable contract could provide opportunity to exceed the initial deposit and offset inflation; however, the market risks must be considered.

Another important decision is to choose an A+ Superior insurance company that can offer this type of investment flexibility, and a consultant that can provide the expertise on structuring such a program for you. Determine how the company will report to the IRS the income generated from the contract and verify that the exclusion ratios are documented in the contract.

An example of a split funded annuity on a $100,000 single deposit plan is shown below.

There are several choices available to develop this type of program. It is generally best to talk with an independent consultant who can review several choices with you.

SINGLE PREMIUM $100,000

	Contract 1 Pay Out Side	Contract 2 Accumulated Side
Issue Amt:	$31,942.00	$68,058.00 (@ 8.0)
Monthly Payments:	625.73	n/a
Exclusion Ratio:	85%	n/a
Value at end of 5 years:	-0-	$100,000.00

32

How Do I Evaluate the Different Variable Annuity Contracts?

by Eric J. Hynden

Eric Hynden is a partner and co-founder of his own independent financial consulting firm. Mr. Hynden's educational background includes a Bachelor of Arts degree in mathematics and economics from DePauw University, a Chartered Financial Consultant's Advanced Degree Candidate from the American College, Merrill Lynch's School of Advanced Financial Management. His background stems from the banking industry to providing extensive consulting services regarding estate and investment issues. Hynden was President of the International Association for Financial Planning of the Greater Fort Myers Chapter in 1991. Mr. Hynden holds a Series 7 license with a registered broker/dealer and also real estate, life insurance, and mortgage brokerage licenses. Eric's diverse background in the financial market makes him a highly respected and sought after speaker.

An annuity is the deferred or accumulation phase in a long-term, tax sheltered savings account. No current income taxes are paid as the earnings accumulate.

Because of this tax deferral, annuities make an excellent savings vehicle for college, second homes, retirement, or any long-term savings goal.

NUMBER OF YEARS		10	20	30
6%	Taxed*	$76,838	$118,083	$181,467
	Tax-deferred	$90,701	$164,532	$298,466
9%	Taxed*	$95,090	$180,844	$343,932
	Tax-deferred	$121,759	$296,506	$722,051

*Assumes 28% tax bracket.

REAL RETURNS

Year	What You Earned*	What You Really Ended up with, after Taxes and Inflation*
1980	+9.59%	5.50%
1981	+11.89	0.34
1982	+12.88	+5.37
1983	+10.33	+3.64
1984	+11.44	+4.29
1985	+11.21	+4.27
1986	+9.60	+5.81
1987	+7.67	+1.12
1988	+9.12	+2.17
1989	+9.13	+1.94

* On long-term Treasury bonds, maturing in 10 years or more. Rate is based on previous year-end figures as reported in the Federal Reserve Bulletin.

** Inflation rates are based on the Consumer Price Index for each year.

The popularity of the variable annuity is that this investment combines the tax advantages of the annuity with the investment return potential of mutual funds. Many have felt the need for higher rates of return in their long-term investing to offset the effects of inflation.

Past tax law changes dealt a heavy blow to the tax advantages of mutual funds by requiring that 90 percent of all interest, dividends, and capital gains be paid out annually. This forces a tax each year on money most people do not wish to receive. An advantage that the variable annuity sub-accounts have beyond the mutual funds, is the simplicity of keeping track of your cost basis for tax purposes. For mutual funds, that process requires extensive record keeping if dividends, interest, and capital gains are reinvested back into the mutual fund at new share prices. For variable annuities, you report only as you choose to receive withdrawals, at ordinary income tax rates in effect at the time. No capital gains or dividends are reported or taxed during accumulation.

Once the decision to use a variable annuity as a savings vehicle is made, there are additional considerations. Equally important will be who to name as annuitant, owner, contingent owner, beneficiary, and contingent beneficiary. Each contract is full of provisions which may seem unimportant, yet may significantly influence the ultimate outcome of your investment. It is because you have so many options that the variable annuity provides you with many opportunities for financial planning. A client must be sure to work with a professional who understands these tools, and the consequences that exist when designing a plan for you.

A large variety of investment vehicles are offered inside the shelter of this annuity plan. We see many of the top money managers combining talents with creative life insurance companies. Your results will depend directly on the investment results or the funds you choose minus expenses. Some of the most popular funds are growth, equity, balanced, growth and income, international equity, international bonds, corporate bonds, government bonds, utility, and money markets. Switching between investments a limited number of times per year is an additional feature. There can be a benefit to switching as this does not cause an immediate tax consequence under the annuity umbrella, as would be the case in your own portfolio. The professional money manager receives a fee to manage each fund, which is included in the fund expenses shown as a percent of the funds' assets. These expenses will vary depending on the size of the fund, complexity of the investments, and efficiency of the fund manager. Most of the variable annuity expenses are fairly well in line with one another.

Another feature to the variable annuity packages which may be automatic, is the ability to dollar cost average. This is usually accomplished by going from a money market account or fixed account to one of the more equity type funds such as a growth fund. A specific dollar amount is moved on a periodic regular basis to reduce the risk of buying into a single market all at one time.

Most variable annuities are set up as flexible annuities which means additional investments can be made into the same annuity during the accumulation phase.

The most overlooked decision and maybe one of the most important decisions, is who to name as owner, annuitant, and beneficiary of the contract. This can be reviewed with your consultant to incorporate planning opportunities as well as favorable investment and tax results. A major difference between mutual funds and variable annuities is the choice of annuity payment options in a variable annuity. While the annuitant is alive, the owner may choose any annuity payment option identified in the contract.

Partial Withdrawals

Partial withdrawals are usually available without surrender penalties. The partial surrender amount varies in each contract but can be as high as 10 percent to 15 percent of the investment value or initial purchase each year. Most variable annuities have early surrender penalties during the first 5 to 10 years on a declining scale. If the owner desires to withdraw more than is allowed under the charge free withdrawal, the income tax consequences of when and how the money may be withdrawn varies. If an annuity payment option is chosen on a nonqualified annuity, and an income stream has begun, a ratio determines how much is taxable interest and what portion is a return of principal, and therefore, not taxable. Any partial withdrawals are taken on a last-in first-out basis (LIFO). This means that withdrawals are considered interest first and taxable by the IRS up to the interest earned.

The IRS has imposed a penalty of 10 percent on any gain if money is withdrawn before age $59\frac{1}{2}$ and does not meet any of the following criteria; death, disability, or systematic payments over your life expectancy. There are several ways to calculate the systematic payments which vary dramatically. In essence, if money is needed before 59½, there is some latitude on how money can be withdrawn without a government penalty.

To see all this work together, let's take a look at a case study:

Mr. Annuity Is 45, 3 Children
Mrs. Annuity Is Age 42

Their objective is to try to retire early. They need to supplement social security and other retirement funds and would like to buy a second home in the mountains. Currently, they are setting aside $20,000 a year into CDs. They are considering purchasing a variable annuity that offers multiple investment choices and will defer all income until they retire.

They have been saving by taking the excess in their checking account and buying CDs to the tune of about $100,000 over the last seven years, and were frustrated at having to pay income taxes each year even though the interest was left to compound. At current interest rates after tax, even with saving $20,000 per year, it didn't appear they were going to have enough to retire comfortably at age 60. By sheltering the earnings each year from taxation, and permitting that to compound with no taxes due, the results would be significantly higher. At 60, this couple would have several options as to how they wish to withdraw income for their retirement years. This is one example where the utilization of a variable annuity will vary based upon your personal objectives for investment, and your choices of ultimate distribution. The Variable Annuity program does offer a guaranteed death benefit. This benefit has offered a nice option for someone who is 65+ and wants to be more aggressive in investing for growth, but can be secured that his or her heirs will get, for example, no less than their original investment plus 5 percent each year. Each contract may vary in the insurance benefit offered. Please be sure to consult a competent professional before completing your decisions on the placement of assets into specific annuity programs.

33

What Is a Person's "Right to Die," and Is a Living Will Necessary?

by Sherri L. Hynden

Sherri Hynden is a partner and co-founder of her own independent financial consulting firm. A cum laude graduate from DePauw University, she received her Bachelor of Science degree in business and economic theory. To add to her financial background, she was hired by a big eight accounting firm in St. Louis, Missouri, prior to relocating to Fort Myers. Mrs. Hynden received extensive Wall Street training from a major international securities firm as a financial consultant. Author of several published articles, such as "Tax Planning and the Charitable Remainder Trust," "Supertrust," and "The Critical Need for Due Diligence in Life Insurance," her excellent accounting background and financial knowledge are invaluable in her career and many speaking engagements. She holds her Series 7 license with a registered broker/dealer and her insurance license.

An unfortunate but good example is the story about Peter who never expected his wife to be in this condition. The accident took place when she was 35. Now at 42, her condition has been proven irreversible and Peter is in the middle of a court battle to allow his wife to "Die with Dignity." Why hadn't Peter's attorney mentioned the "Living Will" when they drafted their estate plan years ago? Did he think they were too young? How could this have happened?

A very important area of proper estate planning involves personal choice decisions. Decisions on life and death are not easily made nor interpreted. As science prolongs life, more and more individuals and their families will be faced with issues involving "death with dignity" and "the right to die." Currently healthy individuals, young and old alike, should think over their wishes, discuss these issues with their family members, physicians and attorneys, and incorporate their wishes into generally accepted, but properly written documents, including a "living will," and "health care proxy."

Many states have adopted living will statutes while other states recognize the living will only by case law. For example, the State of Florida has a specific statute, number 765 entitled "Right to Decline Life-Prolonging Procedures."

The Florida legislature finds that "every competent adult has the fundamental right to control the decisions relating to his or her own medical care, including the decision to have provided, withheld, or withdrawn the medical or surgical means or procedures calculated to prolong his or her life." The statute goes on to include definitions such as "life-prolonging procedure" and "terminal condition." There are additional sections which detail procedures for notifying the physician and preparing the legal documents. Basically, the Living Will allows people to spell out, in advance, their wishes about being kept alive indefinitely by extreme or extraordinary medical care in the event of terminal illness or irreversible injury. For those individuals who are concerned that they may someday be kept alive in a vegetative state against their wishes, not to mention the potentially tremendous cost and burden to the family, a Living Will is essential.

The American Medical Association currently estimates that 15 percent to 20 percent of adult Americans have written a living will. Not only attorneys, but physicians are also discussing living wills with their patients.

New York State has a law, signed by Governor Cuomo on July 22, 1990, which allows an individual to designate a "health care agent." This is a friend or relative who will decide whether medical treatment will be provided. This law allows an agent to act on behalf of a patient who is comatose or who cannot otherwise communicate with doctors. The agent's authority begins only when physicians determine that the patient has lost the capacity to decide about treatment.

Some state laws provide for special instructions about cutting off artificial nutrition or fluid restoration, but must properly specify authority to a given person. Health care providers are obligated to honor the agent's decisions to the same extent as if they were made by the patient. The individual must be mentally competent at the time of appointing his or her health care agent and the agent must make decisions based not only upon the patient's wishes, but also upon religious and moral beliefs. New York became the first state to enact such law since the U.S. Supreme Court decided in mid-1990 that a Missouri family could not order an end to life support for their comatose daughter.

Even if the domicile state of an individual recognizes the validity of "Living Wills," problems can arise with respect to the effectiveness of such documents. Second, because of the increased geographic mobility of the population (particularly the elderly), a person may be stricken with a disability illness or injury in another state while traveling, etc., in which case the "Living Will" may be ineffective. If someone wishes to sign a Living Will, they should seek proper legal advice.

After completing your Living Will, a "dated" copy should be kept by your spouse or guardian, your attorney, your physician and perhaps your child or children. Living Wills entered into your medical records are available immediately if you are brought in for treatment. This is when they are really needed.

If you have already completed a Living Will, like all documents, it is important to review it periodically. Your preferences might change as you get older and your interests may also change as new medical discoveries are made, or laws are restated.

34

How Do We Set and Share Our Goals with Our Advisors?

by Jan Kantor

Jan Kantor is a business consultant and seminar leader whose major goal is "Enhancing Productivity Through People." Mr. Kantor's company, Success Systems, specializes in comprehensie customer relations, management, and sales programs designed to increase profits and sales on behalf of public and private sector companies. Based in Southwest Florida, Mr. Kantor has 25 years of entrepreneurial experience in management, administration, and selling, enabling him to provide results-oriented plans to help control expenses and growth. In addition to implementing plans for companies, Mr. Kantor presents customized seminars and workshops to "help people communicate with people." Targeted at top management and staff levels, topics include management and leadership skills, marketing and promotion, customer relations, attitude and team building, time management, and

sales training. He is a member of the National Speakers' Association and is listed in Who's Who in Professional Speaking. *Mr. Kantor is author of* Inspiring People in the Work Place, *and has been published in numerous Florida publications, including* Florida Today, The Fort Myers News Press, *the* Southwest Florida Business Magazine *and* Naples Daily News.

Financial and estate planning are designed to assist everyone in creating and managing assets to maintain his or her lifestyle, share with relatives, or gift away.

As a business consultant, my work involves helping people achieve their dreams.

In order for dreams to be reached, they must be well thought out: Specific, Measurable, Attainable, Realistic, and Timely.

Many people talk about their objectives in general terms: a big house, lots of money, etc. Consideration must be given to prioritizing these goals. The individual is the designer of these goals. You are solely responsible for your thoughts and actions, and ultimately for your failures or successes.

Perhaps this list of phrases would serve as a way to prioritize your objectives:

Achievement/Accomplishment	Adventure/Challenge
Income/Wealth	Affection/Love/Relationships
Approval/Acceptance	Economic Security
Status/Recognition	Family Happiness
Freedom/Independence	Morality/Integrity
Security/Order	Self-Development
Pleasure/Fun	Religion
Health	Power

Try this, choose the five most important objectives in your life. After doing so, cross out two. Now, prioritize the remaining three.

Typically, a person finds that being specific about what is important to him or her was not as easy as it appeared. But once it's done, one can focus on the goals that will really have meaning in the future.

Attainment of objectives comes in incremental steps. Remember that as a child, crawling preceded walking!

If your first goal was economic security, it may take a planned strategy over a period of years to accomplish. This planned strategy is a part of being realistic about achievements. How many times have we dreamed about a "wish list" of cars, homes, or entertainment items? Planning a realistic, focused strategy will make things happen.

And of course, time is the greatest consideration of all. We have all said, "If I had purchased that land in California or Florida 10 years ago, I would be very wealthy today." Setting time frames to achieve goals creates the urgency which is absolutely necessary for developing *focus*.

Remember that the two-minute warning in football creates some of the most exciting moments of the game. Setting time frames for achievement will give clarity to what you really want, and create a challenge to reach your goal.

Looking at One's "Point of View"

Some people see life as a glass half empty, others half full. Proper planning begins with an optimistic focus on what you feel is achievable. Remember, life is a journey—most people's goal is good health and happiness which extends through the family unit.

The first step is effort. Implementing this responsibility takes time and energy. There are no magic solutions; a very small percentage of Americans inherit future monetary security. The key is to *plan*, and then have the discipline to stick to it!

The Inner You

When was the last time you sat down and reflected about yourself and your family? This is the principle of "self-actualization" or living up to your full potential.

This introspection takes time; think of your family relationships, and the time it took to build that affinity and trust. The same happens as you become aware of yourself, and what you *really* want out of life.

Making Decisions

Often, people do what is "right" based on another person's input. The question, may be, what is important to the client and his or her family?

The discipline of preparing for the future begins with making decisions.

Your top-five priorities form the foundation of goals you would like to set and achieve. Each family member may have a different set of priorities, but that's OK. This begins the process towards the potential goals a family wants to attain.

You should be reasonable in passing along your objectives and be sure you are comfortable that communication is evident.

35

Will My Grandchildren Pay a Generation-Skipping Tax, and Can Avoidance Be Accomplished through Proper Planning?

by Andrew J. Krause

Mr. Krause is a Florida bar board certified estate planning and probate lawyer. Attending the University of Miami in Florida, Andy received his Master of Laws degree in estate planning in 1981; his Juris Doctor cum laude from Thomas M. Cooley Law School, 1980; and a B.S.B.A. in 1977 from Central Michigan University. As author/ lecturer for the Columbus Tax Conference in 1988, Krause addressed "Planning for Change of Domicile" and in 1989 authored "The Florida Homestead Laws: Planning to Maximize Unified Credits" for The Journal of Taxation of Trusts & Estates. *Andy is now serving as a director of the Collier County Estate Planning Council. He is a*

member of the Collier County and American Bar Associations, serves as a Director and President of the Collier County Unit of the American Cancer Society, and serves on the ACS Florida Division Committee on Planned Giving.

Basically, the generation-skipping transfer (GST) tax could be imposed on the value of the property you and your spouse give or devise to your grandchild in excess of $1,000,000. Therefore, the property that your grandchildren may otherwise receive could be reduced by the GST tax, unless you and your spouse employ proper planning.

The GST tax is separate and distinct from the estate and gift tax provisions of the Internal Revenue code. The GST tax was enacted to reduce the benefits of transferring property beyond one generation (i.e., beyond your children to your grandchildren). The legislative policy enables Uncle Sam to take a wealth transfer tax bite (whether the tax is in the form of a gift, estate, or GST tax) out of your property at each generation, as the property descends down through the generations of your descendants.

At your death, your property is subject to estate tax. Thus, Congress has its tax bite at your generation. If you devise your property to your children, the same property or its value (assuming your children do not deplete the property) would be subject to estate tax at the children's deaths. Thus, Congress has its tax bite at the children's generation. However, if at your death, you devise your property directly to your grandchildren, Congress has been robbed of its tax bite at the children's generation. Therefore, in order to prevent this perceived inequity, Congress imposes the GST tax on the devise to the grandchildren to make up for not having the estate tax bite at the childrens' death.

The estate tax $600,000 unified credit exempt amount will not in any way offset the GST tax that is imposed for transferring property beyond one generation. However, every individual is allowed a $1,000,000 GST tax exemption to offset $1,000,000 of generation-skipping transfers. After the $1,000,000 GST tax exemption has been completely exhausted, or if the individual elects not to apply the GST tax exemption, a taxable generation-skipping transfer would occur and would be taxed at the then existing top marginal estate and gift tax rate. The new GST tax is currently the highest in the United States, a flat tax of 55 percent for years beginning prior to 1993. Many wills and trusts are outdated due to the 1986 tax law changes, because prior to this date, assets directed to grandchildren would not have incurred the extra GST Tax.

Proper planning to avoid the GST tax would begin by ensuring full utilization of you and your spouse's $1,000,000 GST tax exemption. This is similar to the way in which proper planning must be employed to ensure full utilization of you and your spouse's $600,000 unified credit exempt amount against estate taxes. Likewise, various estate planning techniques have been developed to leverage the value of the $1,000,000 GST tax exemption which can substantially increase the value of property that may be transferred to grandchildren without reduction for the GST tax. Various planning techniques may also be employed to maximize the value of such GST tax exempt properties for the benefit of your grandchildren and other lineal descendants at generations below your grandchildren.

For example, one of the popular devices used to leverage the value of the $1,000,000 GST tax exemption is the Dynasty Trust or Endowment Trust. Whatever the name, the idea is to create an irrevocable trust for the benefit of descendants that would stay in existence for as long as the law allows (approximately 100 years). You and your spouse could each transfer up to $1,000,000 to the trust and each of you would allocate a like portion of your $1,000,000 GST tax exemption to the trust so that the trust would be completely exempt from the GST tax in the future. Once the GST tax exemption is allocated in this manner, all subsequent appreciation on the trust property would also be exempt from the GST tax; hence the trust property has a "protect" status for GST purposes. The trust would be structured to provide substantial benefits to your grandchildren and lower generations without causing the property to be included in their estates for estate tax purposes. Depending on the needs of the beneficiaries, this trust could be designed to focus on growth for future generations while you, your spouse, and children use other non-protected assets to cover current expenses of the family.

One very effective planning technique is utilization of the $10,000 annual gift tax exclusion for direct transfers to grandchildren. Gifts that qualify for the annual exclusion are not subject to the GST tax. These annual exclusion gifts may even be made in properly planned trusts which escape the GST tax.

There are many other planning opportunities available to reduce the impact of the GST tax. Generally, the complexity of the planning increases proportionately to the increasing impact of the tax on larger estates. One point you should remember is that the GST tax is Draconian in nature and you are well advised to engage proper planning to avoid its harsh impact.

36

How Do We Preserve and Achieve Growth for Our Assets?

by Roger Macaione

Mr. Macaione received his Bachelor of Arts degree in psychology from the University of Connecticut. He was a Capitol area scholar at Trinity College, Hartford, Connecticut. As District Manager for a national investment firm, his duties included recruiting, training, and conducting seminars in the insurance and securities areas. In 1984 he received his Certified Financial Planner (CFP) designation. He has been an NASD Registered Representative since 1977. Mr. Macaione holds his securities, annuities, and life and health insurance licenses. His office is located in Ft. Myers, Florida.

One of the most critical and often overlooked characteristics of a portfolio is investment balance. This term generally refers to the quality of having funds positioned among the three fundamental investment areas in amounts determined by the investor's financial objectives. These three areas are cash oriented investments (savings, money markets, short-term certificates of deposit), fixed return investments (all types of bonds, long-term certificates, annuities, and insurance cash values), and equity investments (stocks, real estate, business ventures). Each area has advantages and disadvantages. Growth and preservation of assets can be reasonably accomplished if you hedge against possible risks, and place investments that are reasonably suited to your objectives.

Some feel that the term "investment balance" has been replaced by the buzzword "asset allocation" or "tactical asset allocation". It has not. Asset allocation seeks to optimally proportion assets among the various subgroups to maximize return and/or minimize risk. These are objectives relating to the mix of assets themselves—to maintaining or growing them. Investment balance, on the other hand, is *investor driven*. A close look at an investor's objectives, as well as the time frame involved in meeting them, is what determines what a balanced portfolio should consist of. Asset allocation models or techniques with all their attendant computer technology can then be applied to some of those assets positioned based on needs.

Numerous investors have pursued many strategies for maximizing return. Some have succeeded, and yet when major financial events have occurred in their lives, they have been unable to respond effectively due to an improperly balanced portfolio. Types of events requiring major asset shifts are children entering college, severe illnesses, and especially, retirement. Just as insurance policies can protect against the unforeseen negative event, a properly positioned asset mix can be available when you need it.

The perspective of balance often eludes an investor and is frequently brought to the investor's attention by a third party—the financial, tax, or legal professional. For many reasons, investors usually don't consider important factors in positioning their funds. It is not rare for the financial professional to meet with the high income individual who is or wants to retire in a few years, but is just embarking on a real estate buying spree for maximum wealth accumulation. Often, retirement is delayed some years until non-liquid real estate is disposed of and the proceeds repositioned in places to provide necessary retirement income. This is a simplistic example, but it is a strong case for you to consider investment balance 10 years prior to your retirement date.

A highly leveraged real estate portfolio, even one appreciating at a wonderful rate, is no help if a business falters or illness strikes, cutting a family's income in half. Other types of investments are needed quickly in a situation such as this. It is amazing how many astute and successful businessmen go on with the inability to muster any cash (aside from borrowing) in a tight pinch. Sometimes leveraged properties and businesses are lost, as valuable as they may be, when funds can't be found.

There are numerous pitfalls inherent in investments themselves. With proper investment balance among the types chosen, these risks remain the only ones which, the investor, you, must deal with. You should never have to worry about making debt payments on a property, whether a dividend or rental check comes in on time, or whether a sizable property can be sold in a short span of time for near market value. Nothing non-liquid should ever be forced to be sold to pay any kind of tax, especially estate taxes of the State or Federal Government. If you find yourself planning on selling these types of assets adversely, you are not balancing your portfolio. The reason is usually the desire for a better return. This motivation for investing usually will wind up taking its toll, not only from liquidity shortages in many cases, but just from the risk inherent in the higher potential. A little thought about your future needs and the timing of those needs, compared to the time frame of your proposed investment, will go a long way in avoiding embarrassing cash flow problems. In addition, find out which investments are sensitive to changes in interest rates. Which are sensitive to inflation? Do they respond positively or negatively when interest rates or the inflation rate goes up? Knowing how these variables affect each investment will help you avoid putting all your eggs in one basket, something critical to financial well-being. A routine annual review with a third party's perspective sought on these points is a good idea. It should be part of your regular, overall financial checkup.

When retired, two primary concerns are: adequate cash flow and accumulated and unused assets earmarked for heirs, hopefully via the most efficient means of distribution available. Sometimes it may be necessary to hold a particularly valuable asset due to pure tax considerations. A piece of highly appreciated and still appreciating real estate might be better off remaining in the estate to give the heirs an increased basis at death. When your heirs sell the property, there may be no income tax liability. The negative of this inaction is that the value can't be converted to income generating investments, and that portion of the estate is not liquid. Proper estate planning can minimize the impact of this investment imbalance.

Protecting your assets becomes the fourth fundamental area to commit funds to. Without adequate protective legal measures and liquid dollar generators, the unbalanced portfolio often caused by retirement will surely create problems with time delay and excessive estate shrinkage. These are common problems lending themselves to usually well-tried and economical solutions.

37

What Is the "Wealth Preservation Trust" and Why Is It Used?

by William H. Myers

Mr. Myers earned a Bachelor of Science degree in business administration from the University of Iowa in 1961. In 1964 he was awarded his Juris Doctor degree from Drake University Law School in Des Moines. His past experience includes 15 years in trust departments of major banks. Admitted to the practice of law in Iowa and Florida, Myers is a member of the Collier County Bar, The Florida Bar, The Iowa State Bar, and American Bar Associations. He has also served on numerous committees as a member of the Real Property, Probate and Trust Law Section of the American and Florida Bar Associations. Since 1978, Bill has concentrated his practice in the areas of estate planning, estate settlement, and trust administration. In addition to his professional activities, Bill dedicates much of his life to civic, community, and religious organizations.

Not long ago, there were many legitimate estate planning options available to pass wealth to our descendants and reduce federal estate taxes. However, in the 1980s massive overhauls and sweeping changes were made to the federal tax system. The phenomenon of no fewer than four major tax acts in the half-decade of the late 1981 to 1986 period can be explained as Congress' response to tighten loopholes and perceived abusive devices. To date, one of the best estate planning opportunities, the irrevocable life insurance trust, frequently termed the "Supertrust" by many financial and estate professionals, has successfully survived the massive overhauls.

Life insurance is undeniably a vehicle with unique attributes. This is particularly true with the advent of modern insurance contracts which provide a competitive investment return. The poorer person may have no other substantial asset to devise, while the entrepreneur's estate may be so heavy in non-liquid assets that payment of taxes, expenses, debts, and cash devises can become imperilled and result in forced sale of assets.

A unique attribute of life insurance is its potential for instant appreciation; no other asset can enhance in value perhaps a hundredfold the very instant after investment. The contingency of this appreciation is not the market demand but the inevitability of death, of which the sole uncertainty is time.

The attribute of instant appreciation, and of income tax-free build-up of cash value coupled with the exclusion of life insurance death proceeds from income taxation, makes the use of life insurance an excellent means of accumulating and protecting wealth. Further, by properly establishing an irrevocable life insurance trust, "Wealth Preservation Trust," to own the life insurance policy, federal estate taxes on the death proceeds can also be avoided and a greater accumulation of wealth can be transferred to your beneficiaries.

If you do not have an irrevocable life insurance trust and are the owner of a policy, then the proceeds are subject to federal estate tax at your death. In "taxable estates," (single in excess of $600,000, or married in excess of $1,200,000, which includes the face value of insurance) as much as 55 percent of the policy proceeds may be paid out in federal estate taxes.

For example, if in 1986 you purchased a $200,000 life insurance policy on your life, and survived your spouse and died in 1991 having a taxable estate of $2,000,000, including the life insurance policy of

$200,000, an additional $90,000 in federal estate tax is generated because the life insurance proceeds are included in your estate. However, if a properly structured irrevocable life insurance trust was established in 1986 to own the life insurance, then the $200,000 proceeds would not have been included in your estate, and thus, $90,000 of estate tax would be saved.

When transferring existing policies to an irrevocable life insurance trust, there are two main concerns for avoidance of estate tax on the policy proceeds at your death: (1) your retention or possession of incidents of ownership in the policy on your life at the time of your death; and (2) the transfer of the policy within three years of death, so that the proceeds become includable in your gross estate. The first problem is not too difficult. If everything goes according to plan, the policy is assigned to the insurance trust together with all incidents of ownership, (i.e., the right to change the beneficiary, the right to borrow against the policy, etc.). However, the second problem is unavoidable. If you transfer the insurance policy within three years of your death, the policy proceeds will be includable in your gross estate and subject to estate tax at death. This three-year rule discourages deathbed transfers of life insurance.

To avoid the three-year waiting period and the concern about possible gift taxes on the transfer, you may establish an irrevocable life insurance trust and allow the trustee to originally procure a new policy. All facets of the application for insurance should be initiated by the trustee, not you. It will still be necessary for you to retain no incidents of ownership over the policy. To ensure you have not indirectly retained any incidents of ownership over the policy, the trust should be administered by an independent trustee (i.e., children, corporate trustee, or other).

The use of an irrevocable life insurance trust can eliminate estate taxes on the death proceeds not only in your estate, but also the taxable estate of the surviving spouse. For example, the trust agreement may provide that the wife is to receive the income for her life, and upon her death, the remaining trust property will be distributed to the children equally. Upon the wife's death, (or husband's death if wife predeceases him), no portion of the proceeds is subject to tax in either estate.

The trust may be "funded" or "unfunded." An "unfunded" irrevocable insurance trust is created by an irrevocable transfer to the trust of only the ownership of the policy. The trustee will have no funds with which to pay the premiums, which therefore must be paid by another (i.e., usually the insured or spouse of the insured). In contrast, the "funded" trust is created by a transfer of cash to purchase the policy plus sufficient funds to be used to satisfy (or to generate income to satisfy) the yearly scheduled deposits to the insurance plan.

In the unfunded life insurance trust, future gifts to the trust for deposit to the insurance plan constitute additional gifts. Often the $10,000 annual gift tax exclusion will completely shelter gifts of premium payments from the gift tax. To this end, certain provisions which authorize your beneficiaries (i.e., wife, children, and grandchildren) to make limited withdrawals from any annual gifts to the trust each year must be included in the trust agreement. Although it is generally expected that these rights will not be exercised, each such beneficiary must be given the right to receive annual notice of trust contributions and of withdrawal rights to qualify the transfer as a gift of present interest.

Because insurance proceeds are often a prime source or liquidity for estate taxes and expenses, it is important for your estate to indirectly retain the source of liquidity provided by policy proceeds. To that end, the trustee of an insurance trust may be granted the discretion to make the policy proceeds "available" to the estate of the insured. For example, the trustee of an irrevocable insurance trust may be authorized to use the insurance proceeds to purchase estate assets (at their fair market value) or to loan funds to the estate (with adequate interest and security). Notwithstanding the trustee's discretion, the proceeds remain excluded from the insured's estate. If, however, the trust instrument directs the trustee to pay debts and taxes of the estate with the policy proceeds, the funds used for such purposes are includable in your estate. In contract, discretionary powers in the trustee allow the policy proceeds to avoid estate tax without necessarily losing the liquidity the insurance provides.

Further tax and non-tax advantages can be enjoyed when the trust is structured not only to benefit your children and grandchildren, but also to avoid estate tax (and generation-skipping tax) at a child's death.

Finally, an irrevocable life insurance trust can be structured to provide your family with the general advantages of a trust, including professional management and investment, especially for minors and incompetents; protection of spendthrift beneficiaries from their own indiscretions or from their creditors; and possible future income tax minimization by the trustee's discretion to distribute income among family members. This estate planning devise has properly earned its respective names, "Wealth Preservation Trust," or "Supertrust."

38

After We Have Set Up Our Living Trust, What Is Necessary to Properly Retitle Our Assets?

by Jill C. Rapps

Jill Rapps graduated with a Bachelor of Arts degree in economics from Potsdam College in New York. She is a member of a network of independent professionals who combine their knowledge and experience for the overall benefit of their clientele. She holds her NASD Series 7 and Series 63 securities licenses, and life and health insurance licenses for Florida and New York, State of Florida Division of Real Estate license, and as a para-planner, provides analysis and servicing for financial programs and estate planning. As a strong advocator of financial education, not only for her clients, but for children and young adults, she is a certified instructor for the National Center for

*Financial Education and a business consultant for Junior Achieve-
ment of Southwest Florida. She is an approved instructor for educational symposiums at the Chautauqua Institute in New York. Jill is the
Naples Coordinator for the International Center for Life Improvement, an organization that evaluates important breakthroughs throughout the world in such fields as medicine, nutrition, learning, and
technology, and is currently a member of the advisory board for TECH
(Training & Educational Center for the Handicapped).*

So few people complete the necessary steps to provide for a probate free transfer of their assets, a major benefit of setting up the
Living Trust. Your assets must be retitled to the name of the trust in
order to be properly "funded." The trust provisions apply only to assets
placed into the trust during your lifetime. If, for some reason, you are
not able to manage your assets, the co-trustee or successor trustee may
step up and do so on your behalf.

In my experience, one of the most important guidelines in funding
trusts is to work with your estate or financial professional because he
or she can assist with a few guidelines that will manage and expedite
this process. We are best equipped to put the items which require
"retitling" together for you and move the process along.

The type of assets that generally are retitled to your executed trust
may include: Real Estate (home/investment), Stocks, Bonds, Mutual
Funds, Certificates of Deposit, Beneficiary on one's life insurance
policies (if applicable), Limited Partnerships, Club Memberships, Business Interests, and perhaps Pension or retirement funds.

The initial process includes drafting a letter of instruction for each
account. This letter should explain the name of the trust, trustee or
trustees of the trust, date which the trust was established, and the tax
identification number of the trust (if it is a Grantor Trust, one in which
you are the trustee for, this is usually your social security number).
Along with the letter of instruction, you should send the pages of the
trust which show the trust name, trustee's ability to transfer the investments into the trust, and the signature pages. This is usually five to six
pages out of the trust. It is generally not necessary to send copies of the
entire trust. If the items you are transferring are stocks, mutual funds,
and tax exempt securities, you will need a guaranteed signature (you

can get this at a brokerage company or a commercial bank). All real estate assets should be handled by the attorney that drafted the trust. In regards to your bank accounts, the letter of instruction and copies of the trust should be sufficient. It is your decision whether your trust name appears on the checks. If you have a large stock portfolio and hold the certificates in your possession, you can set up a brokerage account and transfer your stocks into a trust account. Statements will be sent on a monthly basis reflecting all activity in your account. This process takes less than a week to get into your trust; whereas, if you choose to send the certificates to each respective stock transfer agent/ transfer agents, it could take months. The goal in our firm is to have a client's Living Trust fully funded in 30 to 90 days. When the accounts are transferred to your trust, you should fill out a schedule for accounting purposes. This is usually referred to as Schedule A and is located at the end of your trust. This will help the successor trustee identify assets you have moved into the trust. Each year you should do an annual evaluation as to the description and valuation of the assets in your trust. The one area I have yet to mention is tax-deferred annuity plans. These programs include, IRAs, TSAs, 401(k)s, pension plans, single premium deferred annuities, TIAA-CREFs, etc. These contracts have beneficiary designations that will allow you to automatically avoid probate at the ultimate distribution to your heirs. Also, there are certain tax advantages that are available if you have a named individual as beneficiary instead of your Living Trust.

For example, if both spouses are living and the spouse is the primary beneficiary of the tax qualified plan, upon the passing of the plan owner, the surviving spouse may choose to defer paying taxes by rolling these dollars into his or her name (referred to as an IRA rollover). To leave this tax planning option open, the trust may be named only as the contingent beneficiary. This is an area where you will work closely with your advisor to determine the best options.

Funding a Living Trust does take some advanced planning. Do not turn to your attorney to do this for you because funding your trust is not their specialty. You may find in certain states that many of the investment companies are not yet familiar with Living Trusts and may find it initially confusing to properly title your accounts. The key here is persistence. You will eventually succeed.

Once everything is appropriately funded, you will have peace of mind that you truly have left a legacy for your successors.

39

Who Can Assist Us in Developing Our Net Worth and Cash Flow Statements, and Why Is This Important?

by Chuck Shafer

Mr. Shafer received his Bachelor of Science degree in finance from Florida State University, and has extensive studies in economics, accounting, and statistics. As an established independent financial consultant, with six years of Wall Street training from a major financial institution, his firm specializes in estate preservation with emphasis on tax reduction. Chuck holds his NASD Series 7 license with a registered broker/dealer, Florida Blue Sky Series 63 license, variable annuity license, life insurance, and health insurance licenses, as well as having the opportunity to gain much insight from a family member who is the nation's leading underwriter of Florida municipals. He

*authored "Will Municipal Bonds Remain Tax Free" in the 1989
Vision, a quarterly financial publication. Shafer is a member of the
International Association for Financial Planning of the Greater Fort
Myers Chapter.*

As a professional in the financial services field, I know that we
cannot be supportive of clients' goals unless we first encourage and
assist them in putting all the specific pieces of their financial affairs in
order. The process of revealing financial matters is similar to that of
visiting a new doctor. Let me relay my own personal story.

Some time ago my regular doctor retired and I was forced to do my
homework and research for a local physician I might use. I selected
one who came highly recommended by both his peers and friends. I
was especially apprehensive to go through the unveiling process with
this new physician as I am a very private person.

Gaining trust and comfort levels with someone who wants to know
everything about my body, my eating habits, my personal life in
general, is very difficult. Is it a necessity to share my personal life and
habits if I expect to remain in good health?

It had been nine years since my last physical. I didn't particularly
want to divulge my morning breakfast of two eggs, greasy hash
browns, and several cups of coffee. It dawned on me as I was in the
waiting room that if I didn't tell the doctor about my medical history
and how I have been feeling, he could not advise me properly. As it
turned out, I discussed every minor detail, took several tests, and came
out in great shape, with minor revision to my diet.

There is very little difference when working with a financial
professional who can assist you in putting your assets in proper
perspective. If you want the best advice from the professionals you
work with, be genuine in sharing information so that they may base
their suggestions on a very personalized basis.

Protecting an estate is just as important as building it properly. The
professional will help you layout your financial make-up, including
assets, liabilities, potential future factors that may hinder or promote
financial success. Cash flow is not necessarily taxable or reportable
income only, but it is the first area to review. Coordinating information

with variables in your financial make-up is critical. Begin with who you are, where you are at according to your financial needs and objectives, and where you would like to be. Then find the professional you are comfortable with and have confidence in. They can help see you through the many technical and emotional financial decisions (investment, estate, and tax matters), that you will need to address on a regular basis during your lifetime. Begin with developing your net worth statement and your cash flow. Then plan to take the next step to successful financial independence. An enlightening experience will occur as you develop and monitor your financial progress on at least an annual basis. Your decision-making process will be simpler and more focused and simple because you will be more aware of the details that make up your financial security.

Your financial consultant can provide a more comprehensive overview to completing your net worth statement and cash flow analysis. Use his or her talents to support your own objectives.

40

What Do We Need to Prepare to Complete a Final Estate Tax Return?

by H. Jeffrey Smith

H. Jeffrey Smith graduated from Southern Illinois University with a Bachelor of Science degree in accounting. He received his Certified Financial Planner designation from the College for Financial Planning, Denver, Colorado. He is a licensed Certified Public Accountant in Illinois, Missouri, and licensed, but not practicing, in Florida. He is a member of the International Association of Financial Planners and the American Institute of Certified Public Accountants. Jeff holds insurance licenses in life, health, and variable annuities and his Series 7 NASD license with a registered broker/dealer. After leaving the audit division of Touche Ross & Co. in St. Louis, he became chief financial officer and commercial lender for a St. Louis based bank holding company. Jeff's professional experience continues in Fort

*Myers where he engages in an independent financial consulting practice
with a special emphasis on investment, tax, and estate strategies.*

Filing the final estate tax return is not a particularly enjoyable
process, considering the emotional trauma the surviving spouse has to
endure with all other aspects of the death of a spouse. The following
suggestions will try to simplify the process as much as possible.

Many of life's dramatic moments (i.e., serious illnesses, real estate
purchases), involve a team of skilled professionals. Similarly, the loss
of a spouse and the resulting financial arrangements require the attention
of several professionals. The complexity of asset structure and the
level of lifetime estate planning will largely determine how involved
the post mortem activities will be; however, the following professionals should be involved: CPA or accountant, family attorney, banker,
investment advisor, life insurance agent, family doctor, and various
appraisers.

Each professional will supply information needed to complete the
final estate tax return. The following descriptions clarify the various
roles:

The CPA or Accountant

He or she will file the federal form 706 and assist coordination with
the activities of the other professionals. The form must be filed within
nine months from the date of death. Before filing the return, a good
deal of work must be completed; a full estate accounting must be
prepared. This will require a valuation of all assets and liabilities as of
the date of death.

Income and expenses of the estate must be accounted for up to the
time the estate is settled. Special income tax complications arise
during the time it takes to settle an estate, so special accounting is
required. If a family business is involved, it will have to be valued as of
the date of death. These are just a few of the responsibilities the
executor will have in helping to settle your estate.

The Family Attorney

The involvement of the attorney at the first death hinges primarily
upon how assets are titled and whether there is a will or living trust that

guides the disposition of assets. If probate is required, your attorney must follow tedious and time-consuming filings with the court. If assets are required to transfer to anyone other than the spouse, such as an heir or a trust, your attorney will help determine which assets go where and help you in retitling business or real estate interests.

In the case of assets that pass through a trust vehicle, the attorney's time can be minimized but is still equally important. He or she will advise the surviving spouse on how to handle Family or Credit Shelter Trusts, and file for the necessary Federal ID numbers. The attorney, CPA, and financial professional will have to work together to resolve the many aspects of filing the final estate tax return.

The Banker

The banker will provide a final statement of all bank accounts at the date of death.

The Investment Advisor

He or she will provide a final valuation of invested assets at the date of death, and work with the heirs and other professionals to help them understand the nature of the deceased assets.

The Life Insurance Agent

He or she will settle the death claim on any life insurance policies. Also, if annuities were owned, the life agent will provide an accounting of the annuities as of date of death.

The Family Doctor

He or she will submit all final medical expenses to the estate for payment.

Various Appraisers

All major assets must be appraised as of date of death. These include all real estate, jewelry, and other personal assets.

As in every other aspect of estate planning, each situation is unique and requires customized attention. What is critical in all cases is that your family work with qualified professionals to guide them through the myriad of complexities in closing an estate and completing the required tax reporting. Your situation may involve more or fewer professionals; but, the financial professional will generally mediate as the catalyst of the process, and will work closely with the CPA and your attorney. They will know what services will be provided by each and help to tie up the loose ends so that the surviving spouse or children can spend as little time as possible on the tedious circumstances in completing the necessary estate filings.

Glossary of
Estate Planning Terms

ACCOUNTING: Judicial proceeding to review trustee's transactions.

ACTUARIAL TABLES: Used by IRS to calculate present value of future interests.

ADMINISTRATOR: Individual (or institution) appointed by the court to administer the estate of a person who died intestate (without a will).

ADVANCE DIRECTIVE: A document in which a person either states choices for medical treatment or designates who should make treatment choices if the person should lose decision-making capacity. The term can also include oral statements by the patient.

AMEND: To change, alter, or modify, i.e., to amend a trust or contract.

ANNUAL GIFT TAX EXCLUSION: Right to give $10,000 per person in any one year ($20,000 if your spouse agrees) without any gift tax liability.

ANNUITANT: The person whose age and life expectancy determine an income payment from the insurance company. The death of the annuitant may also cause the payment of the annuity proceeds to the named beneficiary.

ANTENUPTIAL AGREEMENTS: Fancy name for premarital agreement.

APS INQUIRY: Attending Physical Statement from the person's doctor describing treatment, medications subscribed, and general medical attention given to an individual applying for insurance.

ARTIFICIAL NUTRITION & HYDRATION: A method of delivering food and water when a patient is unable to eat or drink. The patient may be fed through a tube inserted directly into the stomach, a tube put through the nose and throat into the stomach, or an intravenous tube.

ATTESTATION: Act of witnessing the signing of a document and subscribing to that document as a witness.

BASIS: Figure used as cost when calculating gain or loss on sale.

BENEFICIARY: Individual named to receive funds from a will, trust, tax-deferred annuity, qualified retirement plan, or insurance policy.

BEQUEST: Personal property left by a will, usually listed on schedule "A".

BESTOWER: Person who makes gift or bequest or sets up trust.

BYPASS TRUST: Trust to permit maximum use of unified, credit by bypassing marital deduction.

CARDIOPULMONARY RESUSCITATION (CPR): A medical procedure, often involving external chest compression, administration of drugs, and electric shock, used to restore the heartbeat at the time of a cardiac arrest.

CHARITABLE FOUNDATION: An entity that is created to benefit charitable purposes exclusively. The entity can be a corporation (usually called a not-for-profit corporation) or a trust. If things are done properly, no income or gains are subject to income tax, because they are devoted to charity.

CHARITABLE TRUST: Trust in which part of the estate of the grantor is dedicated for charitable purposes.

CHARITABLE LEAD TRUST: Trust set up to pay an income interest to one or more beneficiaries and at their death the principal is turned over to a designated charity (or charities).

CHARITABLE REMAINDER TRUST: A trust where one or more individuals receive payments, usually for life (or lives, if more than one individual). When the life (or lives) ends, the trust assets pass to charity. Favorable tax benefits apply.

CODICIL: Supplement to the will whereby the creator adds to, deletes, or changes the provisions thereof.

COMMUNITY PROPERTY: A system of property rights that prevails for married couples in some states. The law varies among each state.

CRUMMEY POWER: Ability of the beneficiary of a trust to withdraw annual exclusion amount in year in which gift to trust occurred (names after party to lawsuit that established power).

CUSTODIAN: Guardian; trustee; one who has custody.

DECEDENT: Person who has died.

DECISION-MAKING CAPACITY: The ability to make choices that reflect an understanding and appreciation of the nature and consequences of one's actions.

DECLARATION: An advance directive.

Devise: Bequeath real estate by will.

Disclaiming: Renouncing a legacy; a key part of what is known as postmortem estate planning.

Discounts for Minority Interests: Relates to valuation for gift tax and estate tax purposes. When a person owns less than a 50 percent interest in a corporation or partnership or investment, and majority control lies elsewhere, the issue is whether a markdown (discount) in valuing the person's interest is appropriate in valuing the interest for gift tax and estate tax purposes.

DNR: Do Not Resuscitate; a medical order to refrain from cardio-pulmonary resuscitation if a patient's heart stops beating.

Donee: Person who receives a gift.

Donor: Person who makes the gift.

Durable Power of Attorney: The right to act on someone's behalf who is absent, incompetent, or disabled and unable to act for themselves.

Estate: Assets and liabilities of an individual at death.

Executor/Executrix: Person (or institution) designated by testator (the creator of the will) to carry out the terms therein.

Family Partnerships: These are partnerships in which at least one member of the family is active in management. Other family members, who also are partners may or may not be similarly active.

Fiduciary: Trust institution (or individual) who has the duty to act for the benefit of another.

Forced Share: Portion of estate of deceased spouse that must, under state law, be inherited by the surviving spouse.

Freezing Values: A strategy to prevent the value of an asset from getting larger, thereby increasing the person's prospective estate. An essential component of the strategy would be to channel the growth to younger members of the family. The freeze opportunity has been curtailed considerably under current law. In addition, the generation-skipping tax has been added to the law, to apply to gifts and bequests to grandchildren.

GST Exemption: Protects $1,000,000 per donor (or $2 million with spouse's consent) from generation-skipping transfer tax.

Grantor: Individual who creates a trust. Also referred to as the settlor, trustor, or donor.

Grantor Retained Annuity Trust: Is a tax-advantaged trust. Example of a GRAT: Donor creates a trust from which an unchanging annuity (example $20,000 a year) is payable to him or her for a specified period (example 10 years). When that period is over, the trust assets pass to Donor's children. The gift is determined under actuarial principles, with the size of the annuity and the period of payment major factors. The longer the period for payments to Donor, the smaller will be the gift. If Donor dies during the payment period, Donor's estate for estate tax purposes would include part, and maybe all, of the trust, depending on how much of the trust assets are required after death to pay the annuity.

GRANTOR RETAINED INCOME TRUST: Generally is meant to be a trust wherein the grantor (the person who set up the trust) gives assets to the trust and retains the right to receive income from the assets during his or her lifetime, but retains no further rights in regards to this trust and the trust may not be revoked.

GUARDIAN: Person designated to have legal care and control over a person or their property. Avoid court appointed guardianships, if possible.

HEALTH CARE SURROGATE: A person appointed by another to make medical decisions for the person appointing him.

HOLOGRAPHIC WILL: Handwritten will (not accepted in all states).

HOSPICE: A program that provides care for the terminally ill in the form of pain relief, counseling, and custodial care, either at home or in a facility.

INCOME: In the context of trusts, income is the cash flow from traditional assets held by the trust. Commonly, it includes dividends, interest, and rent.

INTER VIVOS TRUST: Gift made during the life of the donor.

INTESTATE: Dying without a will. The state law decrees the division of your property, the designation of your children's guardian, and your estate administrator.

IRREVOCABLE TRUST: A trust which once created and executed, cannot be amended or revoked with respect to the majority of the document. Generally not included as part of an estate.

ISSUE: Descendants.

JOINT INSURANCE POLICY: A life insurance contract covering two or more lives. It may be a joint survivorship, with insurance proceeds payable at death of surviving insured, or a joint first-to-die, payable at the first insured's death. Generally, premium payments required are less than a single insured plan as the actuary tables are more favorable when combining two life expectancies under one contract.

JOINT TENANCY WITH RIGHT OF SURVIVORSHIP: Agreement naming two joint owners, specifying when one dies the designated survivor receives the entire property.

LEGACY: Gift of personal property made by will.

LEGAL GUARDIAN: A person charged (usually by court appointment) with the power and duty of taking care of and managing the property and rights of another person who is considered incapable of administering his or her own affairs.

LIFE-SUSTAINING TREATMENT: A medical intervention administered to a patient that prolongs life and delays death.

LIVING WILL: Also called the "right to die" document is a declaration made by a person showing the person's intent to be allowed to die with dignity and to die naturally and allowing the person to predetermine whether or not he desires to have the removal of feeding tubes and other medical procedures withheld or withdrawn.

MARITAL DEDUCTION: Federal tax law provision that allows a surviving spouse to receive the deceased spouse's estate, tax-free (exception for resident alien spouses).

MARITAL DEDUCTION TRUST: Trust qualifying for the federal estate tax marital deduction. Generally the surviving spouse has full rights to principal and income.

MEDICAL EXPENSE EXCLUSION: Must be paid directly to facility or person providing service.

MEDICAL INFORMATION BUREAU: MIB file pertains to a master information database on previous medical history. Inquiry is permissible when applying for life or health insurance.

NONCITIZEN SPOUSE: Subject to limitations on tax-free gifts that may be received and restrictions on marital deduction for estate tax.

PALLIATIVE CARE: Medical interventions intended to alleviate suffering, discomfort, and dysfunction, but not to cure (such as pain medication or treatment of an annoying infection).

PERSISTENT VEGETATIVE STATE: As defined by the American Academy of Neurology, "a form of eyes-open permanent unconsciousness in which the patient has periods of wakefulness and physiologic sleep/wake cycles but at no time is aware of himself or his environment."

PERSONAL RESIDENCE GRIT: This is a tax-favored plan involving an individual's personal residence, whether it be main residence or vacation place. The owner places the residence in a trust, and reserves the use of the residence for a specified number of years. That right is actuarially determined. The longer the period during which the owner keeps the use of the residence, the smaller is the gift. But if the original owner of the residence dies during the reserved period, the residence will be part of his or her estate for estate tax purposes, and no tax advantage is gained.

PER STIRPES: Assets pass among blood lines (i.e., children to grandchildren, no spouses included).

POSTMORTEM ESTATE PLANNING: Reshaping a decedent's estate by disclaimers and other means to achieve a preferred economic or tax position.

POWER OF ATTORNEY: Giving someone the right to act on your behalf in your absence.

PREMARITAL AGREEMENT: Contract, binding in many states, that can affect inheritance rights and other conditions of the marital relationship.

PRESENT-VALUE CALCULATIONS: Determining what money to be paid in the future is worth today.

PRINCIPAL: In the trust context, the bundle of assets that are placed in the trust; the proceeds from sale of those assets, including profits and gains; the new investments made with those proceeds; and additions to the fund via further gifts.

PRIVATE ANNUITY: Plan by which one person transfers property to another in return for the transferee's promise to make annual payments to the transferring person for his or her life.

PROBATE: Timely and public process by which the validity of a will is determined. All assets not designating a beneficiary go through probate.

PROXY: A person appointed to make decisions for someone else, as in a durable power of attorney for health care, also called a surrogate or agent.

POUR-OVER WILL: A will that distributes or "pours over" the assets of the estate to a living trust and the assets are therefore disbursed from the trust to the beneficiaries.

REMAINDERMAN: Individual who receives trust assets at the termination of a trust.

RESIDUARY CLAUSE: Section in a will or trust referring to the remainder of the estate after other stated bequests or property and money have been taken into consideration.

REVOCABLE TRUST: A trust which can be amended or revoked.

REVOKE: To make void, to cancel, to take back or to rescind, i.e., to revoke a trust.

ROLLOVER: Moving lump-sum retirement payment into an IRA.

SETTLOR: The person who creates a trust, also known as the grantor or trustor.

SPRINKLING PROVISION: Discretionary power given to a trustee to distribute income (and principle if authorized) to two or more beneficiaries of a trust.

STEPPED-UP BASIS: Favorable income tax treatment at death. The valuation of an appreciated asset is its new cost basis.

STOCK REDEMPTIONS: A purchase by a corporation of stock owned by a shareholder.

TAX CONTROLLED INVESTMENT: An investment, such as a variable or fixed tax-deferred annuity, where the owner primarily controls when income taxes should be paid on earnings within the contract.

TENANCY IN COMMON: A way to hold title to property that is jointly owned but each person has control over his or her share and can dispose of the property independently of the other.

TENANCY BY THE ENTIRETY: Title to a property where both the names of husband and wife appear on the deed.

TERMINAL CONDITION: In most states, a status that is incurable or irreversible and in which death will occur within a short time. There is no precise, universally accepted definition of "a short time," but in general it is considered to be less than one year.

TESTAMENTARY TRUST: A trust created by an individual under his or her will. All assets go through probate at the person's death and are ultimately placed in the trust.

TESTATOR: Individual making a will.

TIME VALUE OF MONEY: Concept that a dollar today is worth more than, say, $1.05 a year from now.

TRUST: A legal agreement under which assets are transferred to a trustee (self or fiduciary person or company) who manages the assets on behalf of the beneficiaries, (self or others who are named).

Trustee: Person or institution holding legal title to trust property for the benefit of another. In the case of a revocable Living Trust, you may be trustee for the benefit of your spouse or yourself.

Tuition Exclusion: Does not include room, board, books, and the like. Unlimited. Tuition may be paid directly to the educational facility on another's behalf. This form of gift is not considered part of the annual gift exclusion.

Unified Credit: Reduction of $192,800 in the tax paid on gifts and the estate (equivalent to reducing taxable gifts and estate by $600,000).

Uniform Gifts to Minors Act (UGMA): Widely adopted state legislation providing for custodian and a vehicle akin to a trust to protect assets during minority.

Uniform Transfer of Minors Act (UTMA): A law that provides for accounts similar to UGMA accounts except that the child does not gain control of the assets until age 21 (25 in California). Real estate, royalties, patents, paintings, cash, and securities are allowed in these accounts.

Variable Life or Annuity Contract: Offered by an insurance company. Investments can be directed to variable sub-accounts where the performance of the contract is determined by the return on the individual sub-accounts selected.

Ventilator: A machine that moves air into the lungs for a patient who is unable to breathe naturally.

Will: A document used to determine the distribution of all property owned in your home individually at your death, name a guardian for your minor children, and designate an executor for your estate. A will must be proved valid in probate court.

Index

231

ABOUT THE AUTHORS

Loren Dunton is often called "The Father of the Financial Planning Profession" for having founded the International Association of Financial Planners, Inc., the College for Financial Planning, Inc., and the CFP designation which lead to the prestigious Institute of Certified Financial Planners.

Among the many books he has written in the financial field are *Your Book of Financial Planning* and *Financial Planning Can Make You Rich* (Prentice-Hall), *The Financial Planner . . . A New Professional* (Longman), and *About Your Future* (NCFE).

In 1978, he wrote one of the definitive books on retirement planning and aging called *The Vintage Years* (Ten Speed Press).

In 1982, he founded the consumer-education, non-profit organization, The National Center for Financial Education, and in 1991 The Kiplinger Organization chose Loren as one of the 12 men who have done the most for the field of consumers personal finance. In 1992 Career Press published Loren's *Prime Time . . . How to Enjoy the Best Years of Your Life.*

Kim Ciccarelli Banta, CFP, is president and founder of Ciccarelli Advisory Services, Inc., a Registered Investment Advisory Firm in Florida and New York. She is involved in financial education, investment consulting, and advanced estate-planning techniques. A member of the International Association of Financial Planners and The Estate Planning Council of Naples, Inc., Kim holds her real estate, insurance and NASD securities principal licenses.

In 1986, she was written up in *Financial Strategies* magazine for her innovative style in both business management and philosophy. She is a founding member and on the Board of Governors for the International Center for Life Improvement, on the Board of Advisors for the NCFE, and is a faculty member for the special studies programs at the Chautauqua Institute, New York. Kim also provides continuing education conferences for attorneys, CPAs, CFPs, trust officers, and Insurance Professionals and serves as a director for the American Cancer Society Legacy and Planned Giving Committee. Kim and her son, Joseph Dean Banta, are residents of Naples, Florida.